Quick, Easy and Effective
Behaviour
Management
Ideas for the
Classroom

of related interest

Nurture Groups in School and at Home
Connecting with Children with Social, Emotional and Behavioural Difficulties
Paul Cooper and Yonca Tiknaz
ISBN 978 1 84310 528 2
Innovative Learning for All series

Promoting Resilience in the Classroom
A Guide to Developing Pupils' Emotional and Cognitive Skills
Carmel Cefai
Foreword by Paul Cooper
ISBN 978 1 84310 565 7
Innovative Learning for All series

Anger Management Games for Children
Deborah M. Plummer
Illustrated by Jane Serrurier
ISBN 978 1 84310 628 9

Social Skills Games for Children
Deborah M. Plummer
Illustrated by Jane Serrurier
Foreword by Professor Jannet Wright
ISBN 978 1 84310 617 3

No More Stinking Thinking
A Workbook For Teaching Children Positive Thinking
Joann Altiero
ISBN 978 1 84310 839 9

Let's All Listen
Songs for Group Work in Settings that Include Students with Learning Difficulties and Autism
Pat Lloyd
Foreword by Adam Ockelford
ISBN 978 1 84310 583 1

Quick, Easy and Effective
Behaviour Management
Ideas for the
Classroom

Nicola S. Morgan

Jessica Kingsley Publishers
London and Philadelphia

First published in 2009
by Jessica Kingsley Publishers
116 Pentonville Road
London N1 9JB, UK
and
400 Market Street, Suite 400
Philadelphia, PA 19106, USA

www.jkp.com

Library of Congress Cataloging in Publication Data
Morgan, Nicola S.
 Quick, easy and effective behaviour management ideas for the classroom / Nicola S. Morgan.
  p. cm.
 Includes bibliographical references.
 ISBN 978-1-84310-951-8 (pb : alk. paper)
 1. Classroom management. 2. Social skills--Study and teaching. 3. Teacher-student relationships. I. Title.
 LB3013.M666 2009
 371.102'4--dc22

2008024654

British Library Cataloguing in Publication Data
A CIP catalogue record for this book is available from the British Library

ISBN 978 1 84310 951 8

Printed and bound in Great Britain by
Athenaeum Press, Gateshead, Tyne and Wear

Contents

Introduction

Congratulations! By opening this book you have taken your first step towards reducing and preventing difficult-to-manage behaviours in the classroom.

Every teacher knows that teaching children can be difficult and demanding. Without the correct attitude, resources and techniques behaviour problems can disrupt classes, consume the teacher's time and subsequently affect the education and well-being of all the children. Difficult-to-manage behaviours can range from mild disruption to lack of attention and concentration, destruction, hyperactivity and being withdrawn.

The book has been written from many years of personal experience teaching and managing a range of difficult-to-manage behaviours in the classroom. It is therefore not a book about theories, but a book about practical and *do-able* strategies that work and maintain. The book therefore provides quick, easy and effective techniques to help keep children focused on their work and engaged in appropriate behaviour within the classroom. In doing this, it also helps children develop a range of skills for good classroom behaviour. As with most things in life, it must be noted that not all of the strategies and resources included in this book will be suitable for all classes or children. Rather, they can be adapted according to the needs of the children, the classroom, and the teacher.

This book utilises a framework developed by myself called "The 10 R's for Behaviour Management". The 10 R's is a term for a group of strategies that are efficient, effective, "tried and tested" techniques for managing children in the classroom, no matter what the behavioural difficulties are. They aim to prevent the occurrence of behaviour difficulties, but if problems do occur, they aim to quickly re-establish appropriate behaviour.

On a personal note, The 10 R's has been a fundamental process in my teaching since I qualified in 1995. Without the 10 R's I am quite sure that my experience of teaching would have been a less positive one. I hope that you, the reader, will gain as much from the 10 R's as I have and will continue to do.

Setting the scene – creating the 10 R's environment

It is essential to create the right environment for the 10 R's. This is fundamental to their success. Self-categorisation theory (see Witte and Davis 1996) states that people strive to conform to their representation of the group norm. Thus, this produces homogeneity of attitudes, opinions and behaviours. Hence, based on this theory, classroom behaviour can be established on the basis of what the majority of the children are doing and how they are behaving. Therefore, creating the right environment right from the start, i.e. a quiet environment, will basically be contagious. I have established a number of successful techniques for creating the right environment.

1. First contact – it is essential that your first contact with the children is a memorable one. You need to establish respect immediately in a calm, assertive manner and communicate that the classroom is *yours* and has set rules. A useful technique is to greet the children outside your classroom, by standing at the door and welcoming them in. Be in place ready for them as they arrive. The children must line up outside the classroom. Ask each child to enter, *one at a time*, informing them to sit at their desk and complete the set task, e.g. silent reading.

2. Not ready to come into my classroom? It is highly likely that one or two (or maybe more!) children will "test" boundaries, and will not enter your classroom as you want them to, e.g. they may start talking or shouting out, trying to jump the queue, etc. A very useful strategy to manage this is to very promptly and assertively say to the child, "You're not ready to come into my classroom…please wait there until you are ready to come in."

3. Once all the other children are sitting in the classroom, prompt them again on the set task, e.g. silent reading, and praise those who are completing the task well. Also hand out token rewards. Say "Well done child A for reading quietly. I wonder who else I can see reading quietly?" This way the children are more motivated to carry out the task in order to receive the reward.

4. Return to the child whom you have asked to wait outside the classroom, and say to them, "Are you now ready to come into my classroom?" It is highly likely that the child will now be ready and will enter the classroom in a calm and focused manner.

5. Regularly "catch" each child doing the right thing, the right behaviour – praise openly. Children love praise and when they see other children receiving it, good behaviour becomes contagious! Remember the Golden Five Minute Rule (Chapter 9).

6. It is important to establish silence in the classroom at this point. This conveys your credibility at this crucial initial stage. Continue to praise good behaviour openly.

7. Always sit children who have the potential for behaviour difficulties, in particular concentration difficulties, facing towards the teacher. This way, the teacher is able to "catch" both good and difficult behaviour early, e.g. eyes wandering, facial expressions, etc.

8. Immediately nip undesirable behaviour in the bud. Early intervention is essential which is timely and specific, before behavioural problems become too pronounced. When a child begins to display inappropriate behaviours, however small, immediately catch the behaviour before it escalates to a level where it becomes too difficult to control.

9. Inform the class of the day's token and main rewards. Remind them what behaviours you'll be looking for i.e. completed work, good listening.

10. The class is now calm and focused and ready for the first lesson to be introduced.

11. For the first week, repeat this process every time the children enter the classroom throughout the day. The children then know what is expected of them.

12. The position of the teacher in the classroom is key. Stand or sit with your back to a wall in clear view of the whole class to identify appropriate and inappropriate behaviours immediately and respond appropriately. It is impossible to "catch" good behaviour if you are not continually watching for it, so continually scan the classroom, and "sweep" it with your eyes over and over.

13. Never stand or sit with your back to the children. When using a board, write on an angle to have a full view of the classroom. If children queue, e.g. for work to be marked, they should not obstruct the teacher's view of the class.

14. It is very important to never start to speak to the class if any of the children are talking. Wait until you have their full attention (see Chapter 7 *Response*).

The 10 R's triangle

The diagram, the 10 R's triangle, illustrates how creating the right environment, right at the outset, is a necessity for successfully "owning" your classroom and establishing the right context for good, focused classroom behaviour.

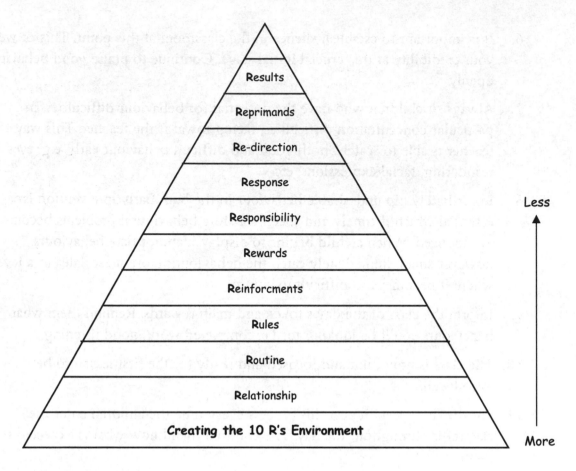

The 10 R's Triangle.

Structuring the 10 R's into this triangle is meaningful as it illustrates how each of the 10 R's relies on its predecessor in order to be effective. Essentially, each one is a foundation for the next. Think of the structure of the triangle as a structure of a house. Each layer is important for building the foundation for the next layer. For example, the first layer of the triangle, Creating the 10 R's Environment, is a fundamental layer. All of the 10 R's rely on it for them to be effective.

The triangle structure shows how the R's at the bottom of the triangle physically take up more space. This is to show that they need to be utilised more than those at the top, e.g. Reprimands. So, more of the bottom-end R's!

The 10 R's

Below is a brief outline of the 10 R's strategies.

1. **R**elationships – this layer of the 10 R's triangle describes the importance of building warm and respectful relationships between the teacher and the children. This is vital for the other strategies to be successful.

2. **R**outine – this layer of the triangle sets out the importance of establishing consistent routines in the classroom.

3. **R**ules – this layer describes the importance of setting up clear rules and boundaries in the classroom, right from the outset. Children actually like rules and rules that enable them to fully understand what is expected of them.

4. **R**einforcement – positive reinforcement is essential for maintaining good behaviour. This layer of the triangle describes how to utilise positive reinforcement for maintaining good behaviour and for changing problematic behaviour.

5. **R**ewards – in the 10 R's, rewards are tangible methods for reinforcing the right behaviour. Similar to positive reinforcement, these are also essential for maintaining and changing behaviour.

6. **R**esponsibility – this describes the importance of teaching children to understand the concept of responsibility and to learn how to take responsibility for their actions. This is vital in helping children learn to self-manage their behaviour.

7. **R**espond – this layer of the triangle describes how to respond to difficult behaviour. Immediate responses are important for efficient and effective management of difficult behaviour.

8. **R**e-direction – in the 10 R's, redirection focuses on redirecting children's energies before difficult behaviour begins. Redirection aims to anticipate potential difficulties and then redirect immediately.

9. **R**eprimands – this is one of the top layers of the triangle, and therefore should only be used once the other R's have been established, and then sparingly. Reprimands are a necessary part of the 10 R's but their place towards the top of the triangle, which means they should be used less, must be noted.

10. **R**esults – the final layer of the 10 R's triangle describes the importance of continually maintaining the results of the 10 R's.

The chapters of this book are organised to address each of the 10 R's in turn.

To complement these strategies, this book also includes handy photocopiable sheets for token and main rewards, and also contains photocopiable plans for daily, weekly and monthly rewards.

1

Relationships

The teacher's skill in managing their class depends on the quality of their relationship with the children. It is essential to start with a new class in the right way by building positive and respectful relationships from the outset.

A teacher must build up trust and friendship with the children as this establishes the basis for behavioural management and change.

Teacher and child

Fundamental to the success of the 10 R's is building strong relationship with the children thereby creating a caring, loyal and respectful bond. This forms a strong foundation from which behavioural change can take place. By displaying acceptance and care for all the children, they then tend to follow by example. There are a number of ways to build a strong and respectful relationship with the class.

1. Be a positive role model for the children, for them to be respectful to others they must be treated with respect.

2. Create a caring, supportive and fair environment where each child feels accepted and that they belong and feel relaxed.

3. Recognise every child's strengths and believe that every child has the ability to learn.

4. Acknowledge, reinforce and share all successes with the class.

5. Involve the children in making decisions regarding rules and activities within the classroom. This helps them to "own" their own rules.

6. Take time to speak to each child individually to find out about their interests, talents, goals, likes and dislikes.

7. Discuss classroom rules and consequences so that all children are clear and understand what is expected of then.

8. When using reprimands (top of the 10 R's triangle) never embarrass or ridicule the children.

9. Interact with the children during play time, enjoy a game of football or just have a chat.

Teacher and parents

The working relationship between teacher and parents can be invaluable when beginning the behavioural change process. Building good relationships with parents can have a beneficial effect on teacher–child relationships, e.g. the children will often absorb their parents' comments and attitudes towards the teacher.

1. Establish a close working relationship with parents to ensure behavioural change success explaining to them what is expected from each child, what the consequences are for inappropriate behaviours and what the reward structure is for good behaviour.

2. Communicate with parents on a regular basis informing them of their child's successes, for example, "Child A was awarded the weekly certificate for improved behaviour in the playground." To maintain communication between both parties use the Home–School Card (see p.52).

3. In the event of a disagreement it is counterproductive to argue with a parent. It is more helpful to not interrupt the parent and allow them to inform you of their problem. Then inform them of your common goal: wanting their child to succeed in school and life.

4. Invite them in to see their child's work, this helps build strong working relationships and builds up respect between teacher, parent and child. If parents do not wish to meet in school (maybe due to negative experiences of their own school days) photocopy samples of their child's work to send home.

5. Always comment positively on the child, regardless of a child's behaviour we all have at least one strength or talent.

You as the teacher

Teaching children and managing sometimes difficult behaviours is not an easy job and can become stressful even for the most accomplished teacher. Think and believe you are a winner and you will win at changing the children's behaviour – Henry Ford said "Whether you think you can, or think you can't – you're right." Positive attitudes are contagious and will affect and change the children's outlook within the class.

1. Believe that you can make a difference, just take your time and use the SMART goals (see p.17).

2. Celebrate all your achievements, however small.

3. Understand that you are only human and you will make mistakes. Remember, mistakes are merely portals to learning.

4. It is important to understand that children's behaviour may only improve slightly or sometimes not at all. It may even get worse before it gets better, which can make us feel helpless, even inadequate.

5. Keep a flexible approach and do what works best for you and the children.

6. Plan ahead, but be flexible and accept change. Remember it takes time to accomplish all your goals. Also, keep your goals realistic.

7. Don't take it personally when sometimes children will not show appreciation for your efforts.

8. If you feel overwhelmed, chat it through with another member of staff.

9. Take time out to enjoy a healthy lifestyle, including exercise, healthy eating and sleep.

10. And, finally, adopt a sense of humour and have some fun!

2

Routine

To help minimise behavioural challenges in the classroom it is important to establish a regular daily structured routine. Most of us function better when we maintain a regular routine and children are no different. Routines help them know what to expect and what is expected of them. Children enjoy routines which are easy to understand and easy to accomplish, yet flexible enough to alter if circumstances change. If there is a change in routine this must be explained immediately to the children so that they are fully aware and have time to adjust.

Morning routine

The morning routine is important to ensure that all children are immediately on track as they enter the classroom. This routine requires practice but the children will soon understand what is expected of them. This creates a productive atmosphere.

The importance of planning and integrating a routine is crucial, although the ability to remain flexible is imperative. During registration inform the children of the day's lessons, events, activities, etc. Inform the children of the day's rewards and what they need to do to achieve them. This helps to keep them focused and motivated.

Afternoon routine

After dinner, inform the children of the afternoon's activities to maintain their focus and motivation. At the end of the day also inform them of the rewards for the following day so that they are more likely to attend school and know what to expect when they arrive the following day.

Using visual systems to communicate the routines of the day is an effective way of helping the children digest them and follow them.

Environment

The atmosphere in the classroom is an important factor to promote appropriate behaviour, with the desired behaviours constantly being reinforced either pictorially or verbally. The following ideas can be helpful in promoting the right classroom atmosphere and environment.

1. Remove anything that could cause distraction.

2. Visual systems listing rules, rewards, consequences and activities.

3. All pencils sharpened, pens working and other stationery made accessible to the children.

4. A designated Time Out and Chill Out area (see p.45).

5. Separate children who disagree with one another by arranging the seating to decrease conflict.

6. Structure lessons into short sessions to help maintain the children's attention.

7. Seat children who experience attentional problems close to you and limit the distractions.

Activity routines – fair selection

Developing a fair selection scheme in the class is vital so that an environment of equality is established. This process eliminates disputes about turn-talking for activities, and therefore avoids inappropriate competitiveness. Discuss with the children the importance of fairness within the classroom. Ask the children to discuss ways in which they can make it fair for children to be chosen to take part in certain activities, etc. Encourage them to create the "fairness rules", and therefore to "own" them.

Effective resources to use for this are lollipop sticks, paper, table tennis balls and containers. Write the names of the children on these items and place each set of names in a designated container, for example:

- Special Day selection, use lollipop stick names placed in a red box, see p.70.
- Eyes at the Back selection, use laminated paper names placed in a blue box, see p.70.
- General selection, write names on table tennis balls and place in a bag.

Choose a child who is behaving well to select a name for a task or activity, and let the whole class know that the child is being chosen because of their good classroom behaviour.

Teacher's planning and goal-setting

Routines are also important for the teacher as they free up more time to be creative, effective and also deal with any problems. Not being prepared and organised usually sets the scene for most discipline problems. The teacher must ensure that all lessons are planned. This way the teacher's attention can be focused on the children's behaviour and time-wasting, which can cause children to become bored and display inappropriate behaviour, is reduced.

SMART goal-setting

Always involve the children when setting goals. Use the SMART method (see below for details) and choose no more than three goals at a time. These three goals should only include one major task and two minor tasks. This way the teacher and child can easily monitor progression and accomplishment. The major task can be made specific to the individual's behaviour and the minor tasks can be generic to the class. Remember that goals need to promote the learning of new skills, see p.19 for an example.

Child's Goals

Write down each child's goals, which can be used alongside the Silver Star Weekly Reward Chart and the Gold Star Monthly Reward Chart (see p.000 and p.000).

Here is an example of a child's goals:

1. *Major task* = a trouble-free playtime.

2. *Minor task* = putting hand up in class.

3. *Minor task* = saying please and thank you.

Teacher's goals

It is very difficult to monitor everything in the classroom. The teacher must therefore prioritise the focus, decide on what to achieve and then evaluate it. This way, the teacher can select the most effective tasks and implement them more often.

Here is an example of a teacher's goals:

1. *Major task* = support each child to ensure a productive and enjoyable playtime.

2. *Minor task* = teaching children to put their hand up in class without shouting out.

3. *Minor task* = teaching children the simple manners of saying please and thank you.

SMART goals

SPECIFIC

Be specific and clearly define what you want the children to achieve: their goals.

MOTIVATIONAL

All goals must be motivational and have meaning for the child. Evaluation of their effectiveness is important to ensure that the child is moving towards the set goals.

ACHIEVABLE

Are the goals you set the children achievable? Goals that move them in small steps towards their rewards are the best to keep them motivated, interested and responsive. To avoid the children losing interest use numerous little rewards, delivered for meeting smaller goals. Work on the "here and now", i.e. short-term goals that work towards a longer-term goal. Measure whether they are meeting their goals or not. If not the goal-setting must be changed. Can the goals realistically be achieved with the resources, support and structure?

REALISTIC

Realistic goals are those that can be achieved, as opposed to unrealistic goals, which are just dreams. For example, don't expect a child who has learned to gain attention by disrupting the class to change overnight. This will not only cause frustration for the teacher, but also for the child.

TIME-BOUND

When do you want the children to achieve the set goals? Some children can't wait very long for rewards, therefore rewards which are small and frequent prove more effective. Three different goals coupled with rewards can be implemented, for example, daily, weekly and monthly rewards may be set for the children to aim for.

Goal-setting bank

Learning	Conduct	Breaktime
To be quiet while others are talking or reading.	To use appropriate anger management strategies.	Behave well towards other children.
To answer one question during literacy/numeracy hour.	To tell the truth.	Keep hands and feet to yourself.
To work independently / stay on task (when? duration?).	To communicate appropriately (e.g. Don't shout out) (when? frequency?).	Tell the teacher immediately if an incident occurs.
To complete (how much?) work in (what lesson?).	To raise his/her hand when s/he wants to answer a question.	Sensibly line up at the end of play.
To show his/her work to the teacher at the end of each lesson.	To look at the teacher when s/he is (what?).	Walk quietly and sensibly to class.
To complete (how much?) work in (what lesson?).	To raise his/her hand when s/he wants to answer a question.	Arrive at class on time.

School	Friendship	Classroom
To arrive for school on time.	To make a positive comment towards another member (name of child) of the group.	To tidy books and equipment away in the correct place.
To arrive at school every day.	To report positively on one thing the group/class has done well each week.	To look after the class pet.
To walk in school.	To take a turn reporting back from a small group.	To fetch the milk and squash.
To show his/her best piece of work to his/her mum/dad every (when?)	To play with (name of child) at playtimes.	To use a piece of equipment appropriately.
To bring his/her PE kit into school on (when?).	To apologise to appropriate person(s) after an incident.	To sit at his/her given place in the class.

3
Rules

A well-structured classroom which promotes learning and creates a predictable atmosphere, reduces unacceptable behaviour and encourages success and self-control has rules.

Successful behaviour management involves an abundance of rewarding rather than giving lots of consequences, and if the reward system is effective then the consequences are significantly reduced. All children *must* be clear on the rules. Rules create clear expectations. These must be reinforced on a regular basis and placed in a visible place on the classroom wall. Do not spend the first lesson with your new class talking about rules and consequences; instead, engage them with a passion for learning, achieving and succeeding within the rules.

Informing staff

When issuing rules, and also rules around rewards and consequences, it is always beneficial to try and ensure that all school staff are aware of them as it is important that the school works as a whole regarding behavioural change. The children are then not confused by other's different approaches. When staff are aware they are usually more than happy to provide the support required, thereby ensuring continuity and more often than not their input provides additional resources. This process becomes more effective if the staff also establish positive relationships with the children. Brief staff regarding the procedures you will use to deal with inappropriate behaviour, i.e. the Red Card (see p.50). Such "whole-school approaches" can be discussed on inset days, after school meetings, etc.

After an incident has occurred it is important that all staff involved meet together and debrief and analyse the incident. It is often easy to forget an unpleasant incident but through analysis there are invaluable lessons to be learned that can help to prevent future recurrences.

Informing children

Brief the children on the rules so that they fully understand the rewards and the consequences. In fact, include them in creating the rules. Preparing the children in advance for what is expected of them reduces frustrations and tension. Keep the number of rules to a minimum as too many rules can overwhelm a child and they then become meaningless. It is important to regularly review the rules with the children. This helps to remind them of what the rules are, what is expected of them and what their goals are. It also provides a good opportunity to amend, add and change rules. Have a regular time-slot for a "rules review", e.g. the same day once a month.

4
Reinforcement

Reinforcement is a concept developed by the famous behaviourist, B. F. Skinner (1974), and fundamental in his theories of human behaviour. Reinforcement basically stipulates that behaviour is more or less likely to occur based on the consequences that follow it. So, if a behaviour is followed by positive reinforcement, that behaviour will be more likely to occur again. All human behaviour can be seen to be governed by schedules of reinforcement.

Reinforcement is one of the most important tools and essential for encouraging change in a child's behaviour. Difficult behaviour cannot change if good behaviour is not acknowledged and reinforced; catch a child doing something right/good, i.e. opening a door for a friend, then reinforce this good behaviour, i.e. praise. Never stop praising! Basically, when a child displays good behaviour, however incidental, remember praise, praise, praise. This positive reinforcement will make the behaviour more likely to occur again. Consistently reinforcing good behaviour is just as important as creating rules and issuing consequences.

A powerful reinforcer of good behaviour is in front of a group, class or whole school. Peers can be a powerful form of reinforcement to aid behaviour change. For example, a child who finds it difficult not to react, walks away from a situation which would usually have caused them to react. This "walking away" behaviour is then reinforced in front of the class, e.g. praise and/or token rewards (see p.54–55).

Reinforcing good behaviour is not only an effective way of increasing good behaviour; it is also a natural way of increasing a child's self-esteem. Children feel good about themselves when they feel that they:

1. feel noticed by others

2. are told what they have done well and rewarded for this

3. feel respected by others through points 1 and 2 above.

When children feel good about themselves they become more inclined to behave better in the classroom. An ideal strategy to increase children's self-esteem is the Special Day programme, see p.70.

Praise

For a child to gain a realistic understanding of their strengths and weaknesses the teacher must provide honest praise and feedback which is genuine, spontaneous and focused on their efforts. This encourages appropriate behaviour, raises self-esteem and confidence. However small a child's efforts, always acknowledge and reinforce. Here are some examples:

- "Well done for opening the door for the class."
- "Thank you for helping child A find his coat, you are a very good friend."
- "I noticed you listened to child A without interrupting."
- "What a kind boy, you played with child A when you saw them on their own."
- "The way you lined up and led the children to class showed great maturity."

For children with severe to moderate behaviour enthusiastic praise and varied vocabulary is important to reinforce acceptable behaviour, for example:

Well done!	**That's terrific!**	**That's amazing!**	**You're brilliant!**
Great work!	**You're brilliant!**	**Wow!**	**Great stuff!**
You're super	**You are clever**	**Fantastic effort!**	**Superb!**

Role-modelling

The teacher must model the desired behaviours they would like to see in the child. Children are like sponges and learn a lot from watching others. So, if a teacher wants the child to tell the truth about a mistake they made they should demonstrate this, e.g. "Sorry child A, I took your pen without asking you first, please accept my apology."

Manners

Manners not only make a good impression on others but also make us feel good about ourselves. As well as opening doors for others and saying "good morning", modelling manners encourages children to treat others with similar respect. Always acknowledge and reinforce when a child demonstrates manners. For example, child A opens the door to allow all their class-mates to pass through. When the teacher passes first they thank the child and in doing so encourage all the other children to do the same. Child A is rewarded with a token and on returning to class asked, "How did it make you feel when all your class-mates thanked you for holding the door open?" This helps the child to understand the feel-good factor they experienced, which they will be more likely to repeat again.

TEAM

The TEAM (Together Everyone Achieves More) reinforcement approach is an effective tool, creating strong clear standards which influence class behaviour. The teacher is just one person and is limited in what they can observe, but encouraging the children in the class to work as a TEAM encourages them to help one another, inform the teacher regarding any issues and provide encouragement and friendship for their peers. When the children work within the TEAM approach, they are unlikely to encourage or provoke any inappropriate behaviour in the classroom and they are less likely to engage in inappropriate behaviours if they see their classmates' disapproval. As a TEAM they must be given a common goal which they can all work towards, for example, a main reward at the end of the day or week for achieving an objective. The achievement of this reward helps reinforce the power of the TEAM creating greater support and strength within the class.

Photo gallery

They say that a picture is worth a thousand words so imagine the impact created by displaying a photo gallery in the classroom of all the rewards, activities, trips, etc. the children have experienced through demonstrating good behaviour. This not only helps to reinforce the child's achievements but also gives them a clear vision of change, confidence and a feeling of well-being. Children who see themselves on view feel loved, valued and special. This also provides an excellent reinforcer for a child who has engaged in difficult behaviour to take time to look at the photos to remind them what they have already achieved.

5

Rewards

Rewards (or reinforcers), when they follow behaviour, make that behaviour more likely to occur again (Skinner 1974). They form the basis of human behaviour and motivation, and can be used effectively to encourage children to acquire skills and develop appropriate behaviour. Rewards encourage positive behaviour, therefore a typical day needs to include a series of rewards to help focus the children. Encourage children to suggest rewards they would like as selecting appropriate reinforcers is not a simple task. If a reinforcer is not reinforcing for the child then it is meaningless. Teachers must continually monitor the effectiveness of the rewards and regularly change them, again, with the input of the children. Establish rewards and consequences that are easy to do and as simple as possible. Effective rewards are those which are attractive, well-timed and conditional.

In summary:

1. Always reward or give positive attention to the behaviours you want to increase and maintain.

2. Immediately reinforce good behaviour with positive consequences.

3. Keep rewards simple, small and frequent to maintain attention and motivation.

Frequency and level of rewards

The frequency and level of rewards given to children depends on the level of behaviour. If a child is displaying frequent and quite difficult to manage behaviour, then the frequency and level of reward must be high. For example, a child displaying severe behavioural problems is not going to respond well to three token rewards and five minutes of free time at the end of the day; instead, they will respond well to frequent token rewards, e.g. 5–10 per lesson and a desirable main reward, e.g. gardening at the end of the day. When the rewards are given and the children start to respond well to the system the reward structure can be revised by raising the standards to qualify for a reward and even reducing the level and frequency of rewards.

Use the diagram below to deliver the correct frequency of token and main rewards:

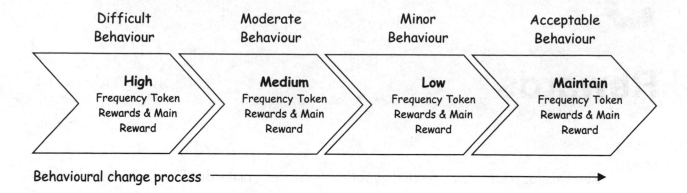

Figure 5.1 *Frequency of token and main rewards.*

Types of rewards

There are two types of rewards:

1. Token rewards.

2. Main rewards.

Remember that a child's attention is changeable, so a reward that is new and interesting one day may not be the next. Therefore be creative and include variety.

Token rewards

Token rewards are a great way to keep children on task as they are collecting tokens for the main reward, e.g. extra play, Top Shop (see p.100). Tokens are a convenient reward as they can be distributed any time, any place, anywhere, thereby encouraging the child to continue or repeat behaviour that is rewarded. Sometimes circumstances prevent rewards being given immediately, like handing out food during a lesson. Using token rewards the teacher can give reward tokens immediately when good behaviour is displayed. When the child has earned enough token rewards they can then "cash in" and be awarded their main reward. For examples of token rewards see p.55.

Main rewards

Main rewards are given to the children as the main reward of the day, week or month. These rewards should be ranked according to their desirability. They include:

1. Tangible rewards.

2. Activity rewards.

3. Social rewards.

TANGIBLE REWARDS

As the majority of children respond to tangible rewards this is a good place to start. Tangible rewards are a quick and effective way to get children to engage in positive and appropriate behaviour. Food is one of the most basic and effective form of tangible rewards. When giving food as a reward it is important to take into consideration nutrition, allergies and also interfering with a child's appetite, i.e. do not give edible rewards too close to dinner time. For examples of tangible rewards see p.56.

ACTIVITY REWARDS

Children enjoy activities like playing games, watching a film, joining the school rugby team, going on a class trip. These can stimulate the child physically and mentally allowing them a channel to release their energies in a positive, enjoyable and controlled setting. For examples of activity rewards see p.60.

SOCIAL REWARDS

Genuine praise has a very powerful effect on children's behaviour. Verbal (social praise) and tactile (non-verbal praise) praise, e.g. smile, pat on the back, are very reinforcing especially when used in front of the child's peers or whole school. Increased praise leads to an increase in academic achievements and a decrease in inappropriate behaviour.

Our voice is a valuable resource and used properly is of great benefit when reinforcing a situation or outcome. Saying encouraging words to a child when they are performing well reinforces good behaviour. A gentle tap on the child's shoulder also provides a positive affirmation to the child as well as providing a powerful reinforcer. For examples of social rewards see p.58.

In summary

1. All rewards should be given *immediately* following the desired behaviour.

2. The teacher must inform the children what specific behaviours will be rewarded.

3. Remember, if rewards are given unsystematically they will lose meaning and have no desired effect.

6

Responsibility

Taking responsibility for one's actions can be very difficult and requires confidence and self-belief. When children learn to take responsibility it helps them to recognise and understand what is good behaviour and what is inappropriate. Teaching children to stop and think about what they are doing and what consequences may result from their actions significantly aids the behavioural change process.

Mistakes

Mistakes can be viewed as portals to learning. As humans we all make mistakes and these should be seen as a valuable and effective way to learn. When a mistake has been made the child must be encouraged to see it as a valuable learning process and helped to decide how to resolve the issue:

> We learn wisdom from failure much more than from success; we often discover what will do by finding out what will not do; and probably he who never makes a mistake, never makes a discovery. (Samuel Smiles)

Telling the truth

Children often fail to tell the truth, make up stories or blame the incident on someone else because they are unsure, or are afraid, of the consequences. Telling the truth is essential to understanding behaviour and to changing it.

In order for the child to feel safe to relay the incident truthfully they must already understand the consequences. This process was addressed in Chapter 3. In addition, the teacher must continually reinforce the message that honesty is a good behaviour and that honesty will not warrant negative consequences (depending on the severity of the incident). For the children to feel confident about this, make it easy for them, e.g. speak to the child in private, and not in front of the class. Inform them that you already know what happened then reinforce that no consequences will be given if they tell you the truth. Reinforce the message that everyone makes mistakes, and that there are consequences for lying. Avoid asking direct and threatening questions. For example, do not ask, "Did you trip child A up?" Instead, ask in a calm voice, "Child A was hurt in the playground, he is very upset, can you tell me what happened?"

When the child tells the truth to the teacher in private, celebrate this with the class. For example, say "Child B made a mistake in the playground this morning, but he told the truth and apologised to child A. I am very proud of him for telling me the truth, so let's give him a big round of applause for telling the truth." Remember, the teacher is reinforcing telling the truth, not the behavioural incident.

Apologise

After a behavioural incident it can sometimes be difficult to empathise and therefore to want to apologise. Timing of apologising (giving the apology and receiving it) is therefore vital. Figure 6.1, the time–intensity model (Smith 1993), illustrates the course of an anger-fuelled behavioural incident. The "recovery phase" following an incident is a risky time to discuss the incident and to start requesting apologies. This is because it is a time when further incidents are highly likely. Therefore, it is important to wait for a child to calm down fully, to get back to "baseline", before discussing the incident or requesting apologies.

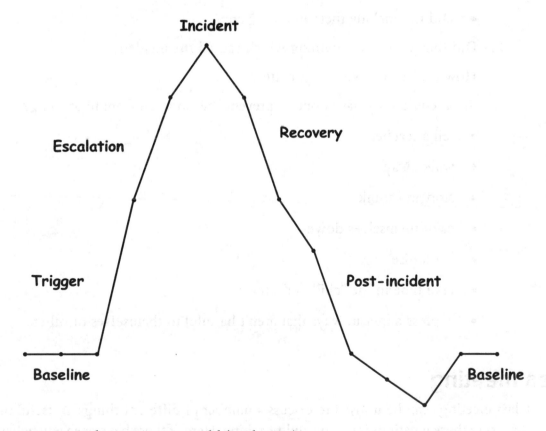

Figure 6.1 The time–intensity model (Smith 1993).

Apologising needs to take place in a quiet area away from other children and adults, and of course, when the time is right for all involved. Remember the time–intensity cycle above.

Stop and think

For a child to learn about taking responsibility they must learn to understand the factors that can lead them to behave inappropriately. Adults regularly find this very difficult, so children will struggle with this even more. It is about learning to take responsibility, as opposed to mastering it. Inform the child that everyone gets angry as it is a natural emotion but it is not okay to hurt yourself or others.

In teaching responsibility regarding behavioural incidents, help the child to identify:

1. How they felt – hurt, angry, frustrated, misunderstood, rejected or afraid?

2. If another child was involved, what did that child do to cause them to react?

   - Did they push them?

   - Used inappropriate language?

   - Take their possessions?

   - Did not include them in their game?

3. Did they do or say anything which caused the incident?

4. How they can make things better?

5. What could they have done to prevent the situation from happening?

   - tell a teacher

   - walk away

   - stop and think

   - calm themselves down

   - apologise

   - take time in the "chill out" area

   - express anger in ways that aren't harmful to themselves or others.

Class meeting

Class meetings can be utilised to discuss a number of different things. A useful thing to discuss in these meetings is responsibility-taking. Here, if there have been any behavioural incidents that week (it is helpful to hold the meetings weekly otherwise the children may forget past incidents) they can be discussed and reflected upon in the meeting *in a non-threatening, non-blaming and reassuring way*. Incidents of good behaviour are also discussed in these meetings, and rewards given. Class meetings need to be a regular occurrence so that the children don't think of them as only occurring in response to a behavioural incident. This would then make the meetings threatening.

The teacher decides what incidents will be discussed in the meeting, usually choosing one or two negative incidents and about two or three examples of good behaviour. All the children are encouraged to comment on the incidents discussed. The child (or children) who were involved in an incident are asked to listen as the class discuss it. The children reflect upon the following, led by the teacher:

1. What happened?

2. What could have led to the incident?

3. How it made the class feel?

4. How could it be prevented from happening again?

5. What can we all learn from this?

Examples of good behaviour are discussed in the same way, but point 4 above is changed to "How could this behaviour be encouraged to occur more often?"

Choice

Encouraging children to make their own choices is another way of teaching responsibility. One example of this is to give the children the choice of what they would like to do for free time each day. Once each child has finished the task in hand they can then get on with their choice for free time. As well as teaching responsibility, this provides a powerful tool in motivating and focusing the children to finish their work quickly in order to obtain the reward.

Jobs

Classroom jobs are an excellent way at providing children with responsibility. Jobs can be allocated in a number of ways, e.g. operating the Fair Selection system (see Chapter 2). Jobs also give children the opportunity to physically move around the classroom as some may find it difficult to sit for long periods of time.

7

Response

Responding correctly to an incident of inappropriate behaviour is vitally important. Always address the behaviour and follow through to gain the child's respect. But before this can happen you must begin to understand what has caused the behaviour to ensure an effective and positive outcome. Always remember to separate the child from the inappropriate behaviour and try hard not to ever take a child's behaviour personally. All children are unique and because of this a "treatment for all" is not the best approach. Instead, children must be responded to according to their individual needs.

Anticipate inappropriate behaviour

Try and "catch" inappropriate behaviour before it starts. Watch for the signs and symptoms, e.g. bickering, sulking, etc. (see Table 7.1). Arrange activities to reduce them. For example, if a child is always reluctant to stand quietly in line after play time talk with the child beforehand, inform them of the token and main rewards in place for that day, convey your expectations and praise when the child completes the task. Always be aware of where the children are and who they are with as this may help prevent inappropriate behaviour from taking place. This helps to reduce opportunities for incidents to occur. Create supervised groups for children with behavioural problems. Always "catch" the right behaviour and reinforce, reinforce, reinforce.

To limit inappropriate behaviour, praise is key. Remember, never stop praising good behaviour. It is always best to focus on increasing positive behaviours through praise and reinforcement instead of trying to reduce inappropriate behaviours. Pro-active behaviour management is the bedrock of good behaviour. However, reactive techniques are also necessary.

Table: Inappropriate behaviour characteristics

Restlessness	Attention-seeking
Boredom	Easily distracted
Disrespectful to members of staff	Inability to tell the truth
Inability to listen to instructions	Passing negative comments
Short concentration spans	Can be physically disruptive
Frustration	Difficulty relating to others
Anxiety	Difficulty responding to academic tasks
Lack of coping behaviours	Excessive behaviours

Remain in Control

It is important to detach yourself from the situation and not take it personally. Attributing the incident to yourself in some way, e.g. "I didn't handle that well; I am not a good teacher", is not helpful as this will only arouse negative emotions and this will be detrimental to both teacher and child. Take a deep breath and display a calm and confident exterior as this may help to reduce the child's anxiety and their frustration so that they feel more secure. This enables them to accept responsibility for their own behaviour.

Only deal with the situation when you are ready to ensure the best possible controlled outcome. Allow the child/children to take time to calm down, e.g. directing them to another room and requesting they return to class when they have calmed down. Remember to reassure them that you care about them and that their display of behaviour has not affected this. Remember to keep your tone of voice low and calm no matter how frustrated or upset you may be.

Also, utilise surprise approaches – some children may predict what your response will be and are ready to react in a certain way. Changing your approach can generate a different outcome which could be of benefit to both teacher and child.

Providing choices

Continuing the teaching of responsibility: children should be encouraged to choose their behaviour and then understand the consequences that follow that choice. It is unhelpful to try and control a child. Instead, enable them to make their own choices, for example, if a child is engaging in inappropriate behaviour, remove them from the classroom and give them a choice whether to continue with the inappropriate behaviour or to try and calm down and return to class displaying a positive attitude. If the child feels not ready to calm down, offer them an alternative to returning to the classroom, e.g. going to a quiet room.

Identify the Reason

It is important to try and identify the reason for behaviours occurring. Remember, all behaviour has meaning and is communicating something. It has a function and it is the teacher's challenge to find this out. Make a list of unacceptable behaviours the child displays then rank them according to importance/severity. If possible focus on the behaviour at the top of the list and reflect on the following over a period of time.

1. Why do you think it happens?
2. When does it happen?
3. When does it not happen?
4. Where does it happen?
5. Who else is involved?
6. How often does it happen?
7. How is the behaviour stopped?

Remember to also think about the child's needs and the role of these needs in the behavioural difficulties. For example:

- needs social attention/interaction
- frustrated
- feels tired
- not very well
- hungry
- too excited
- problems at home
- difficulty dealing with a new situation
- being bullied
- bored
- needs to feel important/special.

Once the functions have been identified appropriate interventions can be applied. Remember behavioural change is a slow process. Children learn how to behave over long periods of time (appropriate and inappropriate behaviour). The child will probably have been practising these behaviours for years and they will need to gradually learn more desirable behaviours to replace the unacceptable ones.

Evaluate strategies

Evaluation is an important procedure to monitor what does and does not work regarding interventions. Evaluation should be carried out on a regular basis to determine if an approach is working. If the approach is not working then new approaches must be introduced – it is a process of trial and error, and requires patience!

Skills training

Some inappropriate behaviours occur as a result of a lack of skills. Therefore, providing children with the necessary skills to enable them to better manage their own behaviour is important, e.g. teaching them decision-making and problem-solving skills. These skills enable them to be more creative and resourceful, giving them feelings of more self-confidence and control. Reflecting on behaviour in class meetings (see Chapter 6) is an ideal forum for this.

Ignore minor misdemeanours

Depending on the severity and the situation, sometimes ignoring a behaviour is a more effective consequence. This is especially useful if the function of the behaviour is to gain attention inappropriately. This is why it is important to understand the function of behaviours.

Humour

Humour is a good method to defuse a situation and also redirect a child's inappropriate behaviour. It can reduce tension, stress and anxiety, stimulating a smile and even a laugh in a difficult situation. Humour is not appropriate for all discipline situations and it should be used selectively.

Positive talk

It is good practice to tell children what you want them to do instead of what you do *not* want them to do. The more positive you are as a teacher the better the results will be. A key study where researchers recorded how many negative and positive responses a child received during one day, demonstrated that, on average, each child received 460 negative or critical comments and only 75 positive or supportive comments (Canfield 1982). This study indicated that the provision of positive responses is a less automatic process than providing negative responses, and therefore giving positive feedback requires focus.

Gaining children's attention

To create a learning environment, gaining the children's attention is paramount. Below are some suggestions on how to gain children's attention.

Token rewards

As soon as the children stop and listen reward them with a token reward which acts as a motivation for the main reward.

Table inspection

This is very effective in increasing focus and attention. At the end of a lesson surprise the children that there will be a table inspection in, for example, 60 seconds, and you'll be checking: under, around and on top of the table, alignment of the table, the way they are sitting and that all books, etc., have been put in their designated place. A mark out of ten is allocated to each table and tokens are awarded. When the class becomes familiar with Table Inspection, choose a child from each table to inspect a table.

Quiet working

When children are working quietly it is easy to gain their attention. One way to create a quiet working environment is to catch a child whispering as soon as the activity has been set. Stop the class and reward that child for whispering with a token reward. Whispering starts to become contagious and by rewarding certain children throughout the lesson, you'll find that the whole class is concentrating on the activity in a quiet and productive atmosphere.

The rhythm game

1. Let the class know that when you want their attention you'll clap a beat and they must copy that beat. When you stop clapping you want their eyes on you and no talking.

2. The children who complete the task are rewarded with the chosen token reward.

3. Make it challenging for the children by clapping more complicated beats.

4. When increasing difficulty levels remember to provide them with challenges that they are able to complete without feeling frustrated otherwise this will have a detrimental effect on their behaviour.

Puzzles/brain-teasers

Write a puzzle or brain-teaser on the board every time the children return to class, this focuses them on finding an answer to the puzzle or question for a token reward. For those children who have difficulty reading, provide the puzzle/brain-teaser verbally. This exercise ensures the children are quiet, focused and engaged before the lesson is ready to begin. The puzzle/brain-teaser usually keeps them quite busy over playtime too!

Magic tricks

To help focus the children on a set task(s) in the classroom, inform them that at the end of the lesson you will show them a magic trick. This can act as a motivator for task focus. When the magic trick has been performed, do not tell them how it works. Rather, encourage them to think for themselves how it was achieved; to problem-solve the trick. This will keep the children very occupied over the break-time, especially those children who find it difficult to behave during playtime. When they return to class ask if anyone has the solution. Those who get it right are rewarded with a token reward. This will motivate the other children for next time. The whole class is then shown how the trick works. When the children can perform the trick independently, as part of a reward structure, they can then perform the trick in front of other classes and teachers, which can boost their self-esteem. It is often the case that the children will return to school the following day with their own magic trick which helps to create a sharing, exciting and focused class.

Teacher says

Teacher Says is based on the same principles as Simon Says, for example "Teacher says touch your nose, Teacher says touch your toes, Teacher says stand quietly."

Clap if you can hear me

When you want the children's attention say "Clap once if you can hear me," those children who are listening will clap once. Then say "Clap twice if you can hear me," then finally, "Clap three times if you can hear me." On the third clap all the children should be paying attention.

Silence all around game

1. Let the class know that when you want their attention you'll say "123321 Silence All Around has begun", the children must then freeze with no talking.

2. The children who freeze the longest complete the task and are rewarded with the chosen token reward. If all children freeze for a set time they are all rewarded.

3. Time the children to see if they can break their best record. If they break the record they can be rewarded with extra token rewards.

Give me five

Let the class know that when you want their attention you'll hold up your hand and say "Give Me Five." Everyone holds their hand up and begin to count down from five to one getting progressively quieter until they whisper "one".

Finally, remember:

Do	Don't
✓ Remain in control	✗ Lose control of the situation
✓ "Catch" behaviour before it starts	✗ Get irritated or angry
✓ Stay calm, take a deep breath	✗ Raise your voice
✓ Maintain eye contact	✗ Be uncaring and distant
✓ Listen carefully	✗ Verbally corner a child, give them a choice
✓ Observe and keep track of the situation	✗ Make threats
✓ Identify the reason/function for behaviour	✗ Condemn the individual's character
✓ Look for the win–win solution	✗ Reprimand the individual in front of their peers
✓ Comment on good/positive behaviour	
✓ Disapprove of the behaviour, not the child	
✓ Ignore minor misdemeanours	
✓ Evaluate what worked well	
✓ Teach the child to self-manage their behaviour	
✓ Remain consistent	
✓ Inform child of day's rewards	

8

Re-direction

It is important to understand that we cannot control a child's behaviour, but we can re-direct it. Everything a teacher does with a child must accentuate the positive not the negative. When a child displays good behaviour pay attention and reward it immediately. The more attention you pay to behaviour the more it will be repeated, so celebrating when the child does the right thing will encourage them to do it more often. Therefore if you don't want to encourage inappropriate behaviour don't spend a lot of time on it but instead re-direct the energy.

Re-directing energy

There is a reason behind every child's behaviour, some are more obvious than others and because of this they react in a certain way to get what they need, e.g. attention, respect. If a child displays undesirable behaviour, re-direct. For example:

1. Shouting out to answer a question – direct the child's attention back to the way they were sitting, quietly with their hand up ready to answer the question. They then get another chance to display the correct behaviour.

2. If a child tends to fidget and disrupt when the books are being handed out for the lesson and is very methodical when given a task – redirect their attention by asking them to hand out the books at the beginning of a lesson.

3. If a child finds it difficult to wait their turn – include them as often as possible during class discussions. This helps to keep them focused and develops their skills in speaking and listening.

Always "catch" the child doing something right so you can emphasise the positive and give them a reward.

Energy management

Children need motivational and dynamic energy for them to achieve desired behaviours and achieve their goals. When recognising and rewarding appropriate behaviour celebrate with high energy, include the rest of the class, teaching assistant, other teachers and non-teaching staff. This energy is addictive and the child is likely to repeat the process.

Do not put energy and time into inappropriate behaviour – deal with the situation in a calm manner, away from others, then re-direct their attention. As soon as the child displays appropriate behaviour celebrate with motivational and dynamic energy. The child will soon appreciate the different energies and act accordingly for a positive outcome.

9

Reprimands

Reprimands are at the top of the 10 R's triangle for a reason. Reprimands should be used sparingly, and much less than the other R's, which focus on reinforcing the right behaviours and teaching skills. If a teacher finds themself having to use reprimands a lot more than the other R's, then the classroom situation requires re-assessment.

When issuing consequences to a child because of inappropriate behaviour, they must not be implemented in isolation. They must be paired with more positive responses and skill teaching. Create clear consequences that are timely, specific, logical, reasonable and fair, with a clear beginning and ending. *Never take away a reward that the child has already earned.* When behaviour "costs" a child, e.g. not gaining (as opposed to taking away) a token reward, the child's unacceptable behaviour often decreases in time. If consequences are given the inappropriate behaviour may be repeated at a different time, just repeat and be patient. Remember, this is a learning process. Be careful with consequences, however. *Avoid taking away a longer-term reward, e.g. a main reward, as this means that the child will no longer have anything to work for.* This can worsen difficult behaviour. Alternatively, if the child is just unable to gain a token reward, they still have more chances to work for token rewards, therefore keeping them motivated to behave well. There may be occasions, however, when main rewards may need to be affected if a child's behaviour is severe.

Children need to have time to adjust to rules and consequences, it is best to start off leniently and gradually progress to firmer consequences, this way they have time to adapt. Starting off with firm consequences can sometimes have an adverse effect on a child's behaviour. Always offer them encouragement and, even for very difficult behaviour, reward children for simply not running away or shouting in protest when they have done something wrong.

The Golden Five Minutes Rule

When you have needed to reprimand a child for inappropriate behaviour, the risk is that the child could then feel that they have "blown it" and then lose the motivation to be good. So, in order to keep the child focused and motivated, implement the Golden Five Minutes Rule. Here, within five minutes of the reprimand, find something to praise the child on. For example, sitting correctly, reading quietly, completing their work, putting their hand up to ask a question. This is very effective at keeping the child motivated to engage in appropriate behaviour.

Severe behavioural problems

Very severe behaviour problems sometimes require a more boundaried approach. Here, a child may not gain a reward because the behaviour is too severe. It is good to discuss such major incidents in class meetings to discourage behaviour of this severity.

An example of a particularly difficult-to-manage behaviour is a child refusing to leave your classroom when requested to do so. This requires a very systematic approach:

1. Walk towards the child you need to leave your classroom and stand to the side of them, slightly behind them.

2. Bend down and in a low and steady tone say, "I'm not accepting this behaviour from you. I would now like you to the leave the classroom and wait outside the door and think about whether you would like to change your behaviour and come back in to the classroom or go down to the head teacher's office."

3. If the child does this, wait a few minutes to give them time to calm, and then go outside the classroom and say, "Well, what is your decision…to change your behaviour and come back in?…or go to the head teacher's office?"

4. The child more often than not chooses to return to the classroom.

5. If (after point 2) the child will not leave the classroom after being requested to do so, either use the class phone (if there is one), or instruct a sensible child to go and inform the head teacher of the situation in order to implement the school behavioural policy.

It is important to acknowledge that there may be times when the school behavioural policy will need to be implemented.

When to reprimand

Early intervention, which is timely and specific before behavioural problems become too pronounced, is essential. When a child displays inappropriate behaviours that require a reprimand, do this quickly and then re-direct immediately before the level of inappropriate behaviour escalates. Using Figure 9.1 always aim to deal with the unwanted behaviour at Level 1 on the scale.

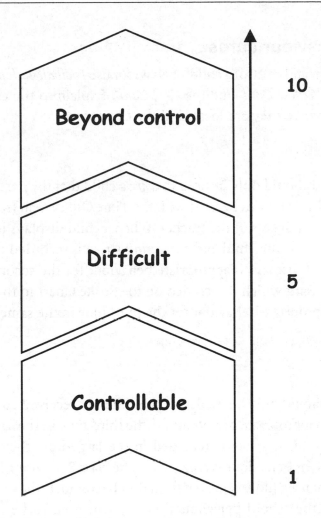

10

5

1

Figure 9.1 Levels of unwanted behaviour.

The teacher must be sincere, excited, firm or warm according to the type of consequences needed. When the child feels that the teacher really means it, the potential for behaviour change is greatly improved. It is important to make your expectations compatible with the child's level of development otherwise they will become frustrated and demotivated

Consequences fail to work

If the consequences are too severe, delayed or inconsistent they will probably fail to work. Start off quite leniently and then gradually increase the intensity until the desired effect is achieved.

Football-style behaviour cards

To help maintain and control a child's behaviour use *Football-style behaviour cards*. There are two types: the *"Yellow Card"* and the *"Red Card"*. Explain to the children the meaning of each card and where they are located in the classroom.

YELLOW CARD

The Yellow Card should only be used to *warn* a child that they are displaying inappropriate behaviour. This card can be used with the Time Out system (see p.45). These cards are located within easy access of the teacher. When a child displays inappropriate behaviour this card is shown to the child and a warning strike is recorded on the Strike Chart (see p.51). If the child displays inappropriate behaviour for the second time they are shown another Yellow Card which is recorded on the Strike Chart in the second small box. On displaying inappropriate behaviour for the third time in the same day the child is shown the Red Card.

RED CARD

The Red Card should only be used after the child has received *two* Yellow Cards. When a child displays inappropriate behaviour for the third time in the same day the Red Card is shown to the child. A strike is recorded in the large box, they are removed from the classroom and their behaviour is recorded in the class Behaviour Book. Follow the above guidance for when a child is removed from the classroom. If they receive three red cards in the same week the school behavioural policy will need to be implemented, e.g. their parents are informed, and they do not gain a main reward.

The verbal 'Five Minutes Card'

An alternative and effective approach to severe inappropriate behaviour is the verbal Five Minutes Card, suitable for children who find it difficult to calm down and deal with situations. When inappropriate behaviour is displayed approach the child and firmly say "You now have five minutes to calm down and turn your behaviour around" then walk away (providing the child and other children are not in danger). The child must be informed that during these five minutes they must calm themselves down then when ready return to you the teacher to discuss the situation. If the child does not return within five minutes they receive a Red Card strike on the Strike Chart, they are removed from the classroom, their behaviour is recorded in the Behaviour Book and they do not gain a main reward.

Time Out

The Time Out system is an effective and widely used approach when dealing with children displaying challenging behaviours. When a child is displaying inappropriate behaviour they are placed in an environment limited in sensory stimulation. Here they can reflect on their behaviour and calm down. The child is given a minute for every year of their age, i.e. if a child is 11 they have 11 minutes of Time Out. This time gives the child the opportunity to calm down and reflect on their inappropriate behaviour and how they can deal more effectively with the situation next time. Time Out is not a punishment but a time for the child to calm down.

Chill out time

"Chill out time" is an effective way for a child to remove themselves from a situation before they react inappropriately. They do this by showing the teacher a Green Card or verbally asking for some chill out time. Designate an appropriate safe area either inside or outside the classroom where the child can go to for one to five minutes to calm down. During this time they can listen to a story tape, read a book, draw a picture or just sit and think. This space can be used pro-actively to prevent behaviours. Alternatively, the space may be used after a behaviour occurs to give the student a chance to re-focus.

This strategy is a very good way of teaching independent self-coping.

Green card

The green cards are given to children who sometimes need time to cool down after a situation has occurred. The cards are either kept in the child's pocket or desk draw and if they need chill out time they present the card to the teacher and go to the designated chill out area.

10

Results

The results of implementing the 10 R's will be evident when you, or anyone else, walk into your class and observe the following:

- calm, relaxed and happy atmosphere
- a child opening the door for the class
- children sitting quietly in their designated seats
- children focused on the teacher
- everyone enjoying playing together during break-time
- the whole class walking sensibly and quietly into assembly
- children raising their hand in order to answer a question
- children working quietly and diligently during lesson time
- incidents being stopped or resolved through self-control
- working as a TEAM (Together Everyone Achieves More).

Most importantly, the 10 R's for behaviour management are not just about developing class management skills for the teacher; they also develop the children's skills in a range of areas. For example, they will have pride in being a member of their class, proud of the work they are achieving, feel more positive about time in school, develop assertiveness skills and develop effective skills in managing their emotions themselves. Long-term, development of such skills in primary school could well have a positive impact on class behaviour in secondary school.

Implementing the 10 R's needs to be ongoing in order to maintain good classroom behaviour. Remember, the child may have been practising inappropriate behaviours for years, so until they have practised good behaviours the whole process must be maintained. As the children and the teacher become familiar with the 10 R's, implementation of them will become more automatic and natural, and therefore require less conscious mental effort from both teacher and children.

Resources

Note on resources

Not all the strategies and resources included in this book will be suitable for all classes or children; instead they can be adapted according to the teacher's/children's requirements.

For those children with more moderate to severe behaviour problems it is important to pay attention to reward systems. Children with more severe behaviour problems often have histories of failing and therefore low self-esteem. Their experiences in life lack positivity and reward, and this has led to them having little reason to behave better. So, positivity and rewards need to be in abundance to show them what is the right behaviour and what is expected of them. Never underestimate the power of just noticing and commenting on the right behaviour. Verbal praise needs to be flowing.

Rewards (such as token rewards) need to be more immediate, more frequent and more varied. Also, goals need to be smaller and very achievable.

Green Cards

Photocopy on green paper, fold in half, stick together and laminate. Green Cards are given to children who sometimes need time to cool down after an incident has occurred.

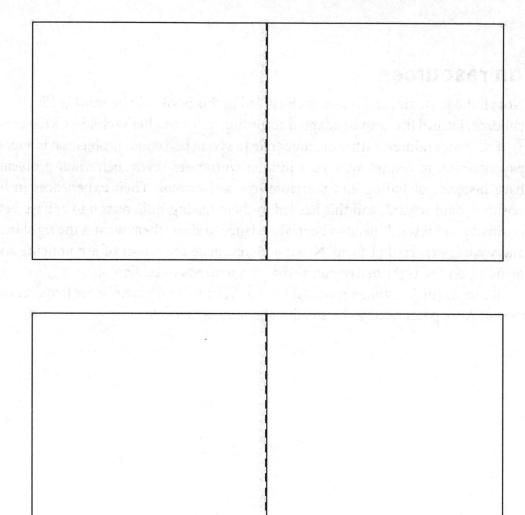

Yellow Cards

Photocopy on yellow paper, fold in half, stick together and laminate. The Yellow Card is used to provide a warning to a child that they are displaying inappropriate behaviour and a warning strike is recorded on the Strike Chart.

Red Cards

Photocopy on red paper, fold in half, stick together and laminate. The Red Card is used after the child has received two Yellow Cards in one day; a strike is recorded in the box on the Strike Chart and their behaviour is reported in the class Behaviour Book.

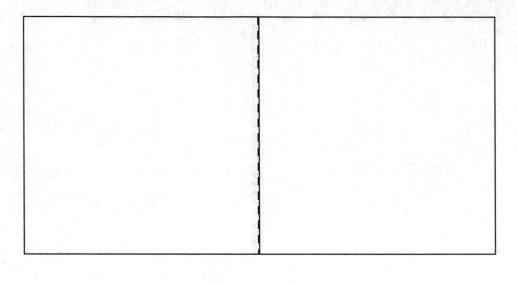

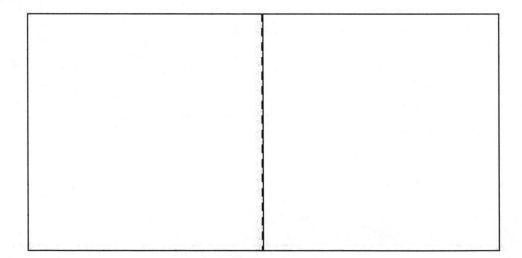

Strike Chart

Yellow and red card strikes are recorded in this chart. If the child receives three red card strikes in a week the school behaviour policy is implemented

Name	Strike 1	Strike 2	Strike 3
	Date: Yellow ☐ Yellow ☐ RED ☐	Date: Yellow ☐ Yellow ☐ RED ☐	Date: Yellow ☐ Yellow ☐ RED ☐
	Date: Yellow ☐ Yellow ☐ RED ☐	Date: Yellow ☐ Yellow ☐ RED ☐	Date: Yellow ☐ Yellow ☐ RED ☐
	Date: Yellow ☐ Yellow ☐ RED ☐	Date: Yellow ☐ Yellow ☐ RED ☐	Date: Yellow ☐ Yellow ☐ RED ☐
	Date: Yellow ☐ Yellow ☐ RED ☐	Date: Yellow ☐ Yellow ☐ RED ☐	Date: Yellow ☐ Yellow ☐ RED ☐
	Date: Yellow ☐ Yellow ☐ RED ☐	Date: Yellow ☐ Yellow ☐ RED ☐	Date: Yellow ☐ Yellow ☐ RED ☐

My Home-School Card

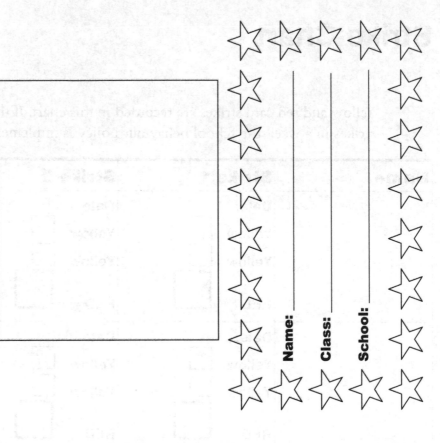

Name: _____

Class: _____

School: _____

Home-School Card

☆ ☆ ☆ ☆ ☆ ☆ Date:

Teacher's comments:

☆ ☆ ☆ ☆ ☆

Parent's comments:

Total Stars:

Total Stars for the week:

Well Done!

How to Use Routines

Date:

☆ ☆ ☆ ☆ ☆ ☆ ☆ ☆

Teacher's comments:

☆ ☆ ☆ ☆ ☆ ☆ ☆ ☆

Parent's comments:

Total Stars:

Date:

☆ ☆ ☆ ☆ ☆ ☆ ☆ ☆

Teacher's comments:

☆ ☆ ☆ ☆ ☆ ☆ ☆ ☆

Parent's comments:

Total Stars:

Date:

☆ ☆ ☆ ☆ ☆ ☆

Teacher's comments:

☆ ☆ ☆ ☆

Parent's comments:

Total Stars:

Date:

☆ ☆ ☆ ☆ ☆ ☆

Teacher's comments:

☆ ☆ ☆ ☆

Parent's comments:

Total Stars:

How to Use Rewards

As discussed in Chapter 5, rewards (or reinforcers), when they follow behaviour, make that behaviour more likely to occur again (Skinner 1974). They form the basis of human behaviour and motivation, and can be used effectively to encourage children to acquire skills and develop appropriate behaviour. Rewards encourage positive behaviour, therefore a typical day needs to include a series of rewards to help focus and motivate the children. Encourage children to suggest rewards they would like as selecting appropriate reinforcers is not a simple task. If a reinforcer is not reinforcing for the child then it is meaningless. Teachers must continually monitor the effectiveness of the rewards and regularly change them, again, with the input of the children. Establish rewards and consequences that are easy to provide. Effective rewards are those which are attractive, well-timed (immediately following the right behaviour) and conditional.

There are different types of rewards, e.g. token rewards, activity rewards, social rewards, etc. The reward you choose will depend on the child, the behaviour and the context. For example, token rewards are very useful for children who are able to wait for main rewards. The tokens provide a very immediate reward which can then accumulate and be exchanged for a main reward (e.g. an activity reward) at the end of the day/week. Children with more severe behaviour difficulties may not respond so well to a token system as waiting might be too difficult for them. Therefore providing a tangible reward (e.g. an activity, an item/object) straight after displaying the right behaviour, as opposed to having to wait through the use of tokens, can be more effective. Overall, adapt the reward system to the learning pace of the child. Examples of different types of rewards now follow.

Token Rewards Guide

- Raffle tickets
- Ink Stamps (The Stamp Trail)
- Caught You Being Good tickets (Caught You Being Good)
- Points chart (Good Behaviour Game)
- Plastic counters (The Safe)
- Plastic money (Top Shop)
- Marbles (Marble Mania)
- Paper Chain Link (Paper Chain Race)
- Paper tokens (see also Star Tokens)
- Stickers

Tangible Rewards Guide (Items/Objects)

Top Shop

Examples:

- Food.
- Drinks.
- Books.
- Stationery.

Collectables

Examples:

- Dinosaur model pieces.
- Football cards.
- Beads.

Stationery

Examples:

- Pens, pencils, rubbers, sharpeners.
- Sketch books.

Sport and exercise

Examples:

- Juggling balls.
- Step counter (pedometer).
- Skipping rope.
- Hula hoop.

Food

Examples:

- Breakfast (toast, fruit, cereal, milk).
- Afternoon snack (milk and biscuit).
- Cakes and healthy snacks (from the cookery activity).
- Fruit and vegetables (from the gardening activity).
- Sweets.

Social Rewards Guide

Praise

For more information see p.23.
Examples:

- From other members of staff.

- Whole-school praise i.e. assembly.

- A smile, nod or wink.

- Pat on the head/back.

- Praise acceptable behaviour.

- Use peers to praise, i.e. during Circle Time, Special Day, etc.

Special Day

For more information see p.70.
Examples:

- First in line.

- Spend half an hour with the class of their choice.

- Free break-time tuck.

- Ten minutes' free time.

- Class jobs.

- Three token rewards.

- Mentor another child, i.e. reading.

Photos

For more information see p.24.
Examples:

- Display photos of children enjoying their main rewards.

- Photos taken by the children.

- Of individual children for their Special Day, p.58.

Children's work

Examples:

- Display child's work around the classroom.

- Send child to show the head teacher their work.

- Stick a special sticker next to good work in their book.

Certificates

Examples:

- For pupil of the week.

- For achieving high marks in a test.

- To inform parents of their child's work.

Activity Rewards Guide

Gardening

Examples:

- Grow vegetables and fruit within the school grounds.
- Mentor younger children and teach them how to grow plants.
- Help maintain the gardening areas, i.e. litter-picking, watering, weeding.
- Paint designs on plant pots to sell at school fete.
- Enter organised gardening competitions.

Cookery

Examples:

- Cook, bake and make cakes, pizzas, healthy snacks.
- Sell products at school fete.
- Enjoy eating what they have made at the end of the day.
- Organise a tea party.

Extra play

Examples:

- Team games, i.e. football.
- Arts and crafts, i.e. sketching.
- Board games.
- Drama.

Free time

Examples:

- Educational games on the computer.
- Listening to music/story.
- Construction sets.

- Model-making.
- Helping in another class.

Computer time

Examples:

- Art and design programs.
- Educational games.
- Internet (if appropriate).
- Design a presentation about themselves.

Games

Examples:

- Board games.
- Computer games.
- Designing and making games.
- Class games, i.e. heads down thumbs up.
- Helping to organise Sports Day.
- Good Behaviour Game, p.92.

Trips

Examples:

- Picnic
- Local park
- Theme park
- Sports centre
- Café
- Activity centre
- Theatre/cinema
- Educational trip.

Jobs

Examples:

- Special Day, p.70.
- Eyes at the Back, p.70–1.
- Teaching the class.
- Helping the teacher.
- Mentoring another child.
- Helping in another class.
- Play leader, member of the school council.

Other

Examples:

- Joining members of staff during dinner time.
- Watch a film.
- Playtime.

The Reward Plan

An effective reward plan will keep the children focused and on task throughout the school year. Except for token rewards, main rewards should always be given towards the end of the day to help maintain the children's behaviour. The following reward types may not be suitable for all classes or children; instead they can be adapted according to the teacher's/children's requirements.

There are five types of reward plans.

Frequent rewards

Given frequently throughout the day to maintain attention, motivation and desire. These rewards are known as "Token Rewards" and can include raffle tickets, plastic money, etc.

Daily rewards

A main reward given at the end of the day when the children have achieved the day's goals through collecting token rewards. These rewards are known as "Tangible" and "Activity" rewards and can include gardening, extra play, etc.

Continuous rewards

These rewards are based on praise for acceptable behaviour and should be given at every available opportunity regardless how incidental the behaviour is. These rewards are known as "Sociable" rewards and can include the Special Day, certificates, etc.

Weekly Rewards

Given at the end of the week when the daily goals have been achieved. The Silver Star Weekly Reward Chart is used to record the children's behaviour or set objectives. For each day there are four small boxes inside one large box. Each small box is ticked after every break-time. If the child has all four boxes ticked they have a silver star sticker placed in the large box. If the child receives five silver star stickers they are eligible for the weekly reward, i.e. watch a film, cake-making.

Monthly rewards

These are awarded at the end of the month when the weekly goals have been achieved. The Gold Star Monthly Reward Chart is used to record the children's behaviour or set objectives. At the end of every week if the child has achieved five silver stars then one gold star is placed on the Gold Star Monthly Reward Chart. If the child has four gold star stickers they are eligible for the monthly reward, i.e. a class trip to the cinema/theatre.

Example Daily Reward Planner

This Daily Reward Planner is based on children with moderate to severe behavioural difficulties.

Day 1

Reward	Type	Time
Token Reward	Plastic Money, p.100	Throughout the day
Main Reward	Tangible Reward = Breakfast Club, p.122	Morning
	Social Reward = Special Day, p.70	Morning
	Activity Reward = Play Time	Throughout the day
	Social Reward = Praise, p.58	Throughout the day
	Tangible Reward = Top Shop, p.100	End of day
	Tangible Reward = Milk and squash	End of day
Reward chart	Silver Star Weekly Reward Chart, p.68	End of day

Day 2

Reward	Type	Time
Token Reward	Paper Tokens, p.112	Throughout the day
Main Reward	Tangible Reward = Breakfast Club, p.122	Morning
	Social Reward = Special Day, p.70	Morning
	Activity Reward = Play Time	Throughout the day
	Social Reward = Praise, p.58	Throughout the day
	Tangible Reward = Gardening	End of day
	Tangible Reward = Milk and squash	End of day
Reward chart	Silver Star Weekly Reward Chart, p.68	End of day

Day 3

Reward	Type	Time
Token Reward	Ink Stamps, The Stamp Trail, p.83	Throughout the day
Main Reward	Tangible Reward = Breakfast Club, p.122	Morning
	Social Reward = Special Day, p.70	Morning
	Activity Reward = Play Time	Throughout the day
	Social Reward = Praise, p.58	Throughout the day
	Tangible Reward = Extra Play! p.120	End of day
	Tangible Reward = Milk and squash	End of day
Reward chart	Silver Star Weekly Reward Chart, p.68	End of day

Day 4

Reward	Type	Time
Token Reward	Caught You Being Good Tickets, p.91	Throughout the day
Main Reward	Tangible Reward = Breakfast Club, p.122	Morning
	Social Reward = Special Day, p.70	Morning
	Tangible Reward = Cookery	Afternoon
	Activity Reward = Play Time	Throughout the day
	Social Reward = Praise, p.58	Throughout the day
	Tangible Reward = Eating food cooked	End of day
Reward chart	Silver Star Weekly Reward Chart, p.68	End of day

Day 5

Reward	Type	Time
Token Reward	Raffle Tickets, p.80	Throughout the day
Main Reward	Tangible Reward = Breakfast Club, p.122	Morning
	Social Reward = Special Day, p.70	Morning
	Activity Reward = Play Time	Throughout the day
	Social Reward = Praise, p.58	Throughout the day
	Tangible Reward = Prize Draw	End of day
	Tangible Reward = Milk and squash	End of day
Reward chart	Silver Star Weekly Reward Chart, p.68	End of day
	Gold Star Monthly Reward Chart, p.69	End of day

Silver Star Weekly Reward Chart

Name	Day 1	Day 2	Day 3	Day 4	Day 5

Gold Star Monthly Reward Chart

Name	Week 1	Week 2	Week 3	Week 4
	☆	☆	☆	☆
	☆	☆	☆	☆
	☆	☆	☆	☆
	☆	☆	☆	☆
	☆	☆	☆	☆
	☆	☆	☆	☆
	☆	☆	☆	☆
	☆	☆	☆	☆
	☆	☆	☆	☆
	☆	☆	☆	☆

Special Day

The Special Day programme provides a positive start to each day and an ideal way to reinforce all the positive behavioural changes each child has made. Imagine having 10–30 children in the class saying something positive about one child, the effect is amazing in boosting self-esteem and, more importantly, acts as a powerful reinforcer for good behaviour. This is suitable for both large and small classes.

Before this programme is implemented the children are taught about compliments, including the different types of compliments, reasons why they are given and how to respond when given a compliment. Different types of compliments are:

- Things a child is good at, e.g. "You have very neat handwriting".

- How a child looks, e.g. "You always dress smartly".

- The way a child behaves, e.g. "You are very kind".

Aims

- Help maintain and improve focus and behaviour in lessons.

- Understand the process of complimenting one another and receiving a compliment.

- To improve self-esteem and respect for others.

- Encourage positive discussions regarding each child.

- To take it in turn to talk and listen when others are talking.

- Special Day and Eyes at the Back gives a structure to the class when lining up, eliminating fussing and disruptive behaviours.

- Develop TEAM work (Together Everyone Achieves More).

What you need

- Special Day box containing names of children.

- Special Day badges designed by the children.

- Eyes at the Back box containing names of children.

- Eyes at the Back badges designed by the children.

- Special Day Passport.

- Photograph of every child.

What to do

1. Every morning during registration a chid is chosen to select a name from the Special Day box, see Fair Selection p.16.

2. The chosen child stands in front of the class and in turn the children, including the teacher, are given a question and then makes one to three positive comments about the child for example:

   - "What do you like about child A?"

   - "What do you think child A's greatest achievement has been?"

   - "What did you miss about not seeing child A yesterday?"

   - "Why is child A such a good friend?"

3. The Special Day child accepts each compliment by saying "Thank you".

4. The positive comments can be written up for the child to take home.

5. The Special Day child is then asked to compliment themselves, e.g. something they are proud of.

6. The child chooses their Special Day badge and is presented with the Special Day Passport, this passport allows them certain privileges for the day; here are a few examples:

   - Spend half an hour in a class of their choice for the afternoon.

   - Has their photo displayed, e.g. on the interactive white board..

   - Always first in line.

   - Chosen for class jobs.

   - Five minutes' free time.

   - Three token rewards.

   - Mentor another child, e.g. for reading.

7. The Special Day child then selects a name out of the Eyes at the Back box. The child selected chooses the Eyes at the Back badge and throughout the day stands last in line and informs the teacher of all the children who line up and walk correctly, e.g. to assembly.

8. At the end of the day a certificate can be presented to the child to congratulate them on a great day, e.g. as a class helper, mentor.

Tips

1. To complement this activity the children can draw around the Special Day child on a large sheet of paper, attach the sheet to a wall and take it in turns to write positive comments down on strips of coloured paper which can be stuck on the child's outline. This acts as a visual reminder for the child and can have a powerful impact. It also reinforces positive behaviour.

2. Each child writes a positive comment about each child in their group/class. These comments are collated so that each child has a sheet with a list of positive comments about themselves. The sheets can be laminated, framed or reduced in size to fit in their wallet or purse which they can read at any time.

3. Encourage the children to compliment other children and members of staff throughout the day. For example, compliment the school cook for preparing their meal. Reward children who do this.

4. If time allows encourage the children to compliment the person sitting next to them.

Special Day Badge Designs

These designs can either be worn as badges or a medal-type necklace.

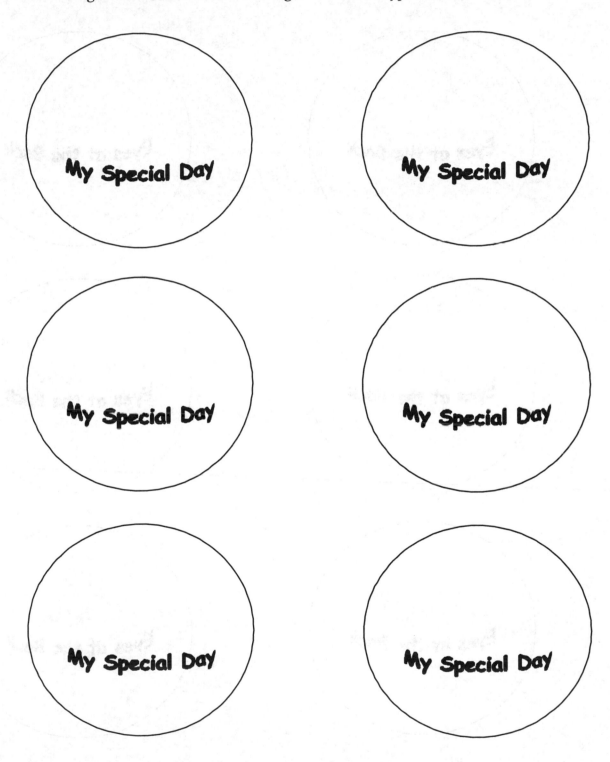

Eyes at the Back Badge Designs

These designs can either be worn as badges or a medal-type necklace.

Eyes at the Back

Eyes at the Back

Eyes at the Back

Eyes at the Back

Eyes at the Back

Eyes at the Back

Special Day Passport Cover

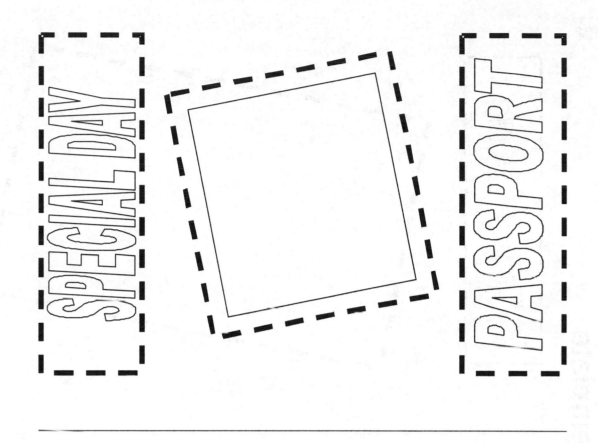

Special Day Passport Page Template

Today I can:

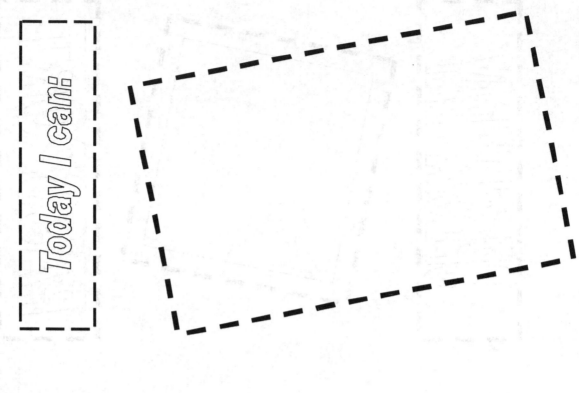

Net for Special Day Box

Photocopy on A3 coloured card.

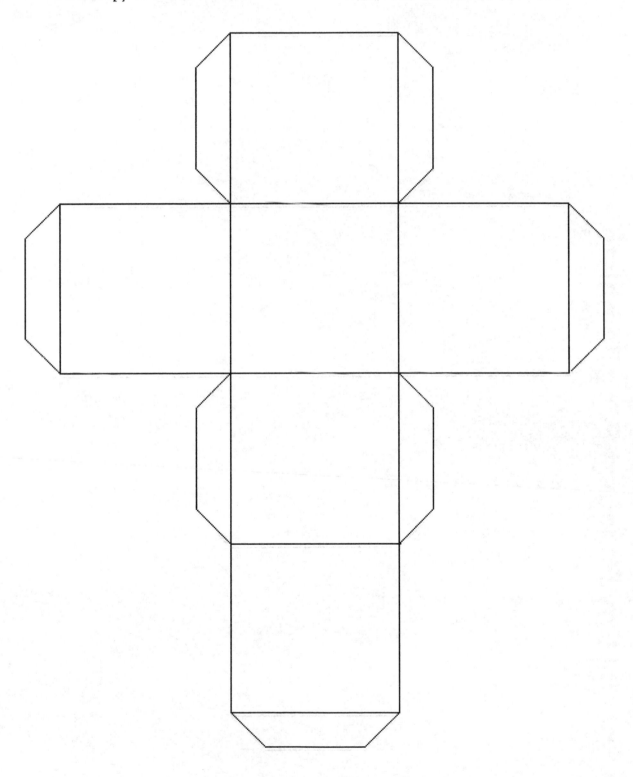

Net for Eyes at the Back Box

Photocopy on A3 coloured card.

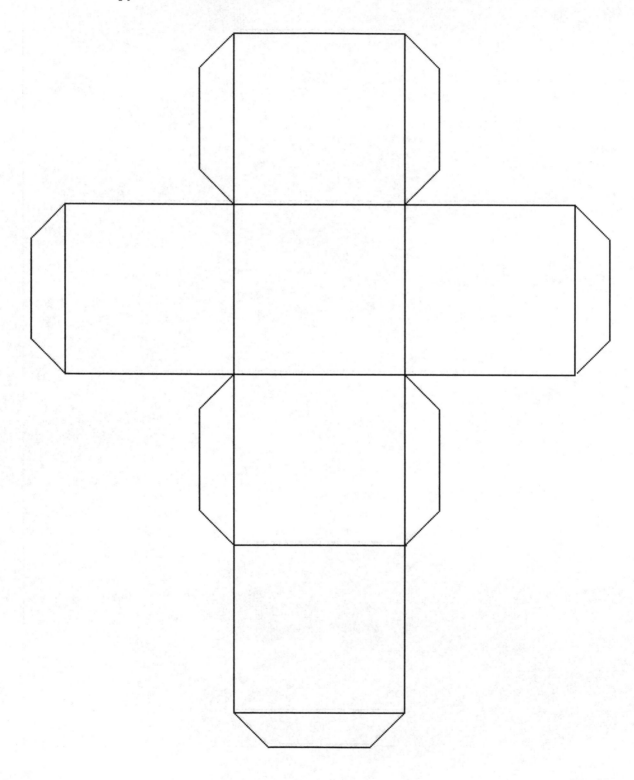

Special Day Certificate

✓

My Special Day Certificate

Awarded to

_____

for

_____

From:_____ Date:_____

You're a Star

Raffle Tickets

The Raffle Ticket reward scheme is very popular with classes of all sizes and levels of behaviour. The children experience the "feel-good factor" knowing that the more raffle tickets they receive the greater the chance they have of winning. According to the class behaviour raffle tickets can be used just for a day (moderate to severe behaviour) or for a week (mild behaviour). This resource works particularly well in managing a large class with a few mild to moderate behaviour difficulties.

Aim

Help maintain and improve focus and behaviour in lessons.

Suitable for

Classes of all sizes and levels of behaviour.

What you need

- Photocopied raffle tickets.
- Box for the children to post their raffle tickets.
- Prizes.

Rules

1. Reward with raffle tickets for every positive behaviour you witness; however incidental it may be, reward it!

2. Decide how many tickets equal the prize.

3. If the child displays inappropriate behaviour:

    - They do not receive a raffle ticket at that time. When you witness good behaviour again reward it immediately with a raffle ticket and lots of praise.

    - If the child has not received enough tickets, they are excluded from the prize draw.

What to do

1. Photocopy a bundle of raffle tickets which can be used to reward the children.

2. Reward good behaviour with a raffle ticket:

    *   When you collect the children from the playground inform them of the prize draw and if they walk correctly to class and sit down quietly they will be given, e.g. two raffle tickets.

    *   At the beginning of each lesson inform the children how many raffle tickets they will be awarded for completing each task.

    *   Before the children leave the classroom for playtime inform the children that walking quietly, lining up correctly and good behaviour will be rewarded with raffle tickets.

3. When a child receives a raffle ticket they write their name on it and place the ticket in the designated box.

4. Either display the prizes for the children to see or place them in a bag to create mystery.

5. Inform the children that the more raffle tickets they are rewarded the greater the chance they have to win.

Tips

1. Do not include just one of a certain item for the prize, e.g. a pencil case, as this will cause frustration for the children. Instead differentiate the first, second and third prizes by awarding an additional item, for example a pencil case and two pencils for first, a pencil case and one pencil for second and a pencil case for third.

2. Always give the rest of the class a small prize, e.g. a rubber or sweet, as they have all worked hard during the day and therefore must be rewarded for their efforts.

Sample Raffle Tickets

Raffle Ticket

Name:

Raffle Ticket

Name:

Raffle Ticket

Name:

Raffle Ticket

Name:

Raffle Ticket

Name:

Raffle Ticket

Name:

Raffle Ticket

Name:

Raffle Ticket

Name:

The Stamp Trail

The Stamp Trail is an effective way to keep children on task by stamping their themed sheets to get them closer to achieving their target and reward. This reward scheme is very popular with classes of all sizes and levels of behaviour. It is also an ideal way to keep a child focused during one-to-one sessions. This resource works particularly well in managing a small group of children, e.g. ten children with mild to severe behavioural problems.

Aim

To maintain the children's behaviour and help focus them on tasks set throughout the day.

Suitable for

Classes of all sizes and levels of behaviour. Small groups of children use the ten stamps per session. For larger groups of children use the four stamps per session.

What you need

- Photocopied Stamp Trail sheets, one per child.
- An ink stamp (if not available the teacher can sign or mark each circle).
- Main reward.

Rules

1. If the child displays inappropriate behaviour:

   - They do not receive any more stamps at that time, but reward for future good behaviour.

   - If the child hasn't received enough ink stamps, the end of day reward will be lost.

2. Reward stamps for every positive behaviour you witness, however incidental it may be, reward it!

What to do

1. Choose a main reward for the end of the day. Try to keep the same reward on the same day every week as this will help to focus the children, e.g. gardening every Tuesday.

2. Decide how many ink stamps equals the main reward.

3. Reward good behaviour with an ink stamp:

    *   When you collect the children from the playground inform them of the main reward (at the end of the day, week or month) and if they walk correctly to class and sit down quietly they will be given i.e. two ink stamps.

    *   At the beginning of each lesson inform the children how many ink stamps they will be awarded for completing each task.

    *   Before the children leave the classroom for playtime inform the children that walking quietly, lining up correctly and good behaviour will be rewarded with an ink stamp.

    *   The Stamp Trail is divided into four sections. The first section runs up to first play, second section to dinner time, third section to last play and fourth section to reward time. This system keeps the children focused and on task throughout the day.

Tips

1. Each Stamp Trail sheet has a different theme, for each theme the teacher can explain the process as a story, e.g. the knight and the treasure trail.

2. Photocopy blank Stamp Trail sheets and have the children design their own which can then be used with the class.

Stamp Trail 1

Name: _____   Date: _____

Find the Treasure!

START!

85

Stamp Trail 2

Name: _____   Date: _____

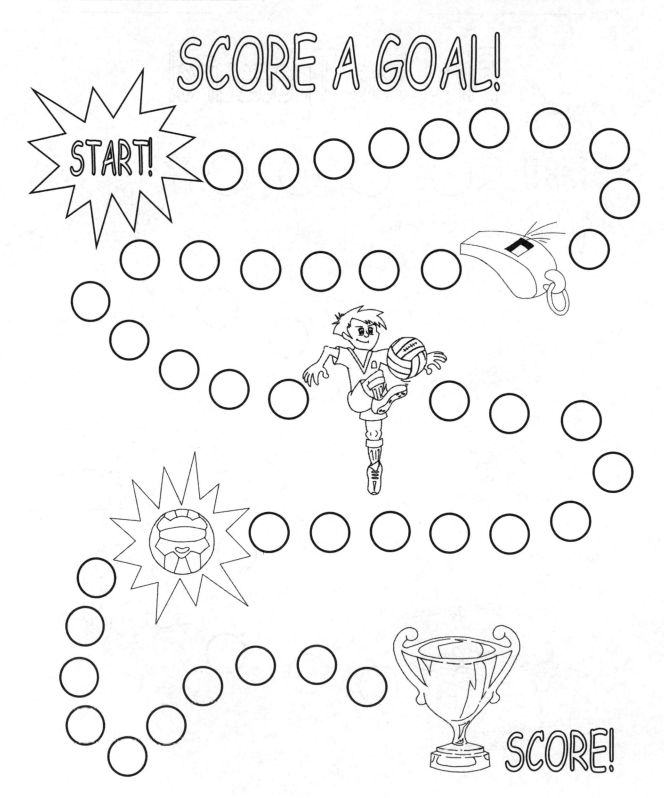

Stamp Trail 1 Template

Name: _____   Date: _____

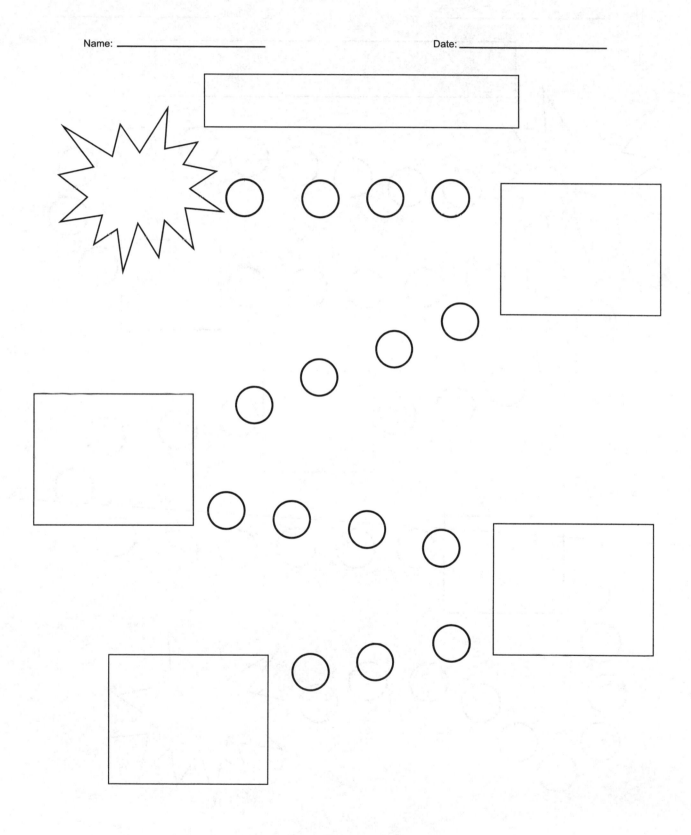

Stamp Trail 2 Template

Name: _____   Date: _____

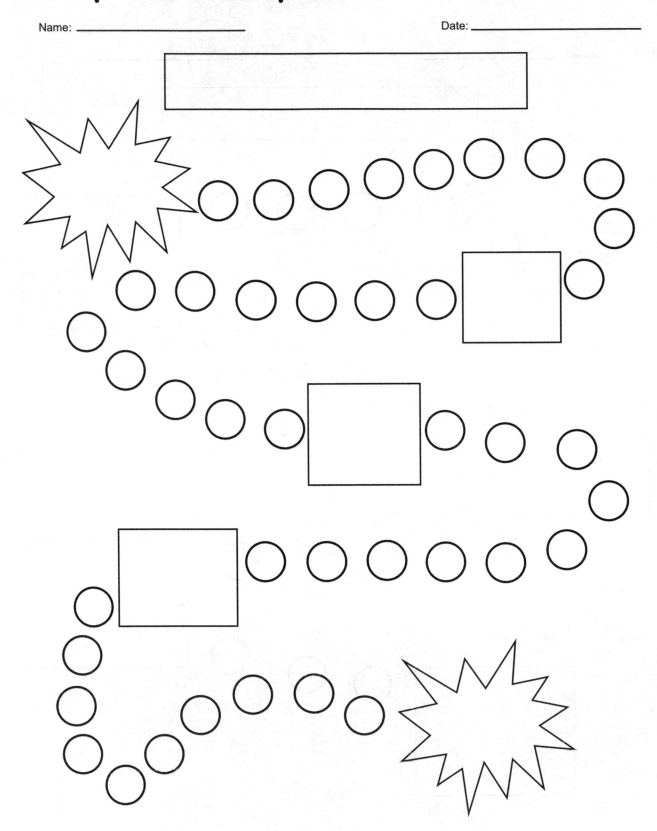

Caught You Being Good!

This is a great way to reinforce positive behaviours. The children experience the "feel-good factor" knowing that they are being recognised for positive things. This technique is suitable for classes of all sizes and levels of behaviour. According to the class behaviour and size this technique can be used just for a day (moderate to severe behaviour) or for a week (mild behaviour).

Aims

- Help maintain and improve focus and behaviour in lessons.
- To help the children identify good behaviour.

Suitable for

Classes of all sizes and levels of behaviour.

What you need

- Photocopied Caught You Being Good tickets.
- Box to place the tickets in.
- Main reward.

Rules

1. Reward Caught You Being Good tickets for every positive behaviour you witness; however incidental it may be, reward it!

2. If the child displays inappropriate behaviour:

    - They do not receive any more Caught You Being Good tickets.
    - If they have not received enough tickets, they are excluded from the end of day main reward.

What to do

1. Photocopy a bundle of Caught You Being Good tickets which can be used to reward the children.

2. Reward good behaviour with a Caught You Being Good ticket. Decide on the number to achieve in order to get the main reward:

   • When you collect the children from the playground inform them of the main reward (at the end of the day, week or month) and if they walk correctly to class and sit down quietly they will be given a Caught You Being Good ticket.

   • During each lesson reward the children with Caught You Being Good tickets when appropriate.

   • Before the children leave the classroom for playtime inform the children that walking quietly, lining up correctly and good behaviour will be rewarded with Caught You Being Good tickets.

3. When a child receives a Caught You Being Good ticket they write their name on it and place the ticket in the designated box.

4. Inform the children that the children who receive x amount of Caught You Being Good tickets receive the main reward at the end of the day/week/month.

Tips

1. Children can reward their peers with the Caught You Being Good tickets providing they give a valid reason. For example, child A is playing on his own and child B asks him to join in with her group game. Child A can reward child B for this act of kindness.

2. Always give the rest of the class a small prize like a rubber or sweet, as they have all worked hard and therefore must be rewarded for their efforts.

Caught You Being Good Tickets

Caught You Being Good

Well done _____

You were caught being good today.

Caught You Being Good

Well done _____

You were caught being good today.

Caught You Being Good

Well done _____

You were caught being good today.

Caught You Being Good

Well done _____

You were caught being good today.

Caught You Being Good

Well done _____

You were caught being good today.

Caught You Being Good

Well done _____

You were caught being good today.

Good Behaviour Game

This is another great way to reinforce positive behaviours, where once again the children experience the "feel-good factor" knowing that they are being recognised for positive things. This is suitable for classes of all sizes and levels of behaviour. According to the class behaviour and size this game can be used just for a day (moderate to severe behaviour) or for a week (mild behaviour).

Aims

- Help maintain and improve focus and behaviour in lessons.
- To target behaviours that need to be improved.
- Develop TEAM work.

Suitable for

Suitable for classes of all sizes and levels of behaviour.

What you need

- Good Behaviour Game Chart.
- Timer.
- Main reward.

Rules

If a child misbehaves during the game, use the following gradient of responses:

- Place them in a separate team. If the behaviour continues:
- Change the type of game and only reward for positive behaviour. If the behaviour continues further:
- Remove the child from the class.

What to do

1. There are two types of games which can be played according to the severity of the children's behaviour.

   - Severe behaviour:

     ○ To help reinforce appropriate behaviours reward points for *good behaviour*, e.g. remaining seated during a lesson, putting hand up to ask a question.

     ○ The team who have achieved x amount of points win.

   - Moderate/Mild behaviour

     ○ To help reinforce appropriate behaviours give crosses for *unacceptable behaviour*, e.g. shouting out, leaving seat without permission.

     ○ The team who have achieved the least amount of crosses win.

2. Tell the children how to play the game.

   - All teams can win if they collect x amount of points/crosses.

   - Review acceptable and unacceptable behaviours and write them on the board.

   - For a large group of children divide into four or more teams, for a small group of children divide into two teams. The children are asked to name their team and the names are written on a chart/board.

3. Always pay special attention to reward points consistently for appropriate/inappropriate behaviour.

4. Play this game for no more than two hours per day. For children with severe behaviour play the game for 10 minutes per lesson throughout the day. At the end of 10 minutes when the timer goes off, the teacher should review with the class how well they have done; remember to praise.

5. When giving marks stick to the Good Behaviour Game rules and teams must not receive crosses for poor academic performance.

6. The winning teams receive a main reward at the end of the day.

Tips

1. To keep the game fresh and exciting you can:

   - Combine crosses (for unacceptable behaviour) and ticks (for acceptable behaviour). A cross deducts one point from the total score and a tick is worth one point. At the end of the game all ticks are added up and the total crosses are deducted.

- Use a large version of the Stamp Trail one per team (see p.83). When good behaviour is displayed a tick is placed in the circle. The winning team is the team which reaches the finish first.

Good Behaviour Game (Individual)

Name

Good Behaviour Game (Team)

Team Name

The Safe

The Safe is an effective tool for one child with behavioural difficulties. According to the child's level of behaviour The Safe can be used just for a day (moderate to severe behaviour) or for a week (mild behaviour).

Aims

- Help maintain and improve focus and behaviour in lessons.
- To help focus a child with severe behavioural problems.
- Develop TEAM work.

Suitable for

Large and small groups of children. Individual children with severe behavioural problems.

What you need

- Toy money box safes or secure money boxes with a lock or combination lock.
- White and red counters.
- Main reward.

Rules

1. Give white reward counters for every positive behaviour you witness; however incidental it may be, reward it!

2. If the child displays inappropriate behaviour they do not receive a counter at that time, but when you witness good behaviour again reward it immediately with a counter and lots of praise.

What to do

1. Say to the children:

- Explain to them that if they collect x amount of points they will receive a main reward towards the end of the day. Place the safe away from the children not to cause distraction.

- When they display appropriate behaviours, however small, reward them with a white counter to place in their locked safe. A white counter is worth one point.

- If they display inappropriate behaviour the teacher will place a red counter in their safe. This red counter cancels out a white counter.

- If the child displays appropriate behaviour at the end of the day they are given the combination to the safe, they must count how many white counters they have and subtract any red counters. The results are recorded on The Safe sheet.

2. For groups of children:

- Place them into teams, each team has a safe which can be placed in the centre of the table.

- The safe can be used as part of:
  ○ The Good Behaviour Game (see p.92).
  ○ Token rewards (see p.55).

Tips

1. Keep a handful of counters in your pocket so that children with behavioural problems can be rewarded at any time.

2. Remember to reward and praise frequently.

3. To maintain the child's attention introduce more counters which are worth different points, for example:

- White = 1 point.

- Blue = 2 points.

- Yellow = 3 points.

The Safe Tally Sheet

Name: _____

Date: _____

The SAFE

Monday   Tuesday   Wednesday   Thursday   Friday

Total:

Top Shop

The shop is an exciting way to keep children on task by earning plastic money for good behaviour and then at the end of the day spending their money on treats from the class shop. This type of reward is ideal for small class sizes, e.g. ten children; and it is very effective in dealing with children with severe behaviour problems.

Aims

- Help maintain and improve focus and behaviour in lessons.
- To help improve the children's understanding of money.

Suitable for

Any child who understands the value of money. Small class sizes, e.g. ten children.

What you need

- Plastic money.
- Plastic bank money bags.
- Toy shop till.
- Items for the shop, e.g. milk, fruit, books, biscuits, pens, etc.

Rules

1. Once money is given to the child it must immediately be placed in the money bag and then in their tray or pocket, this can be reinforced by awarding the child more money when they have stuck to the rule.

2. If the child displays inappropriate behaviour:

    - The shop reward can be foregone.

    - They do not receive plastic money for a lesson/task.

3. Reward money for every positive behaviour you witness, however incidental it may be, reward it!

What to do

1. Choose the same day every week for shop reward as this will help to focus the children.

2. Reward good behaviour with the plastic money:

    *   When you collect the children from the playground inform them that it is shop day and if they walk correctly to class and sit down quietly they will be given, e.g. 50p.

    *   At the beginning of each lesson inform the children how much plastic money they will be awarded for completing each task.

    *   Before the children leave the classroom for playtime inform them that walking quietly, lining up correctly and good behaviour will be rewarded with plastic money.

3. Shopping List sheet, see p.103.

    *   Before last break write up the shopping list on the board and hand out the Shopping List sheets.

    *   The children calculate how much money they have, what they want to buy and how much change they will be given by the shop keeper.

    *   A child's name is selected from the box (see p.16) to be the shop keeper.

    *   Two children at a time are allowed into the shop, then return to their tables and enjoy their rewards.

4. When the children are familiar with the shop reward give them the responsibility of organising and setting up the shop.

Differentiation

Less ability:

1. Tokens can be used instead of plastic money, e.g. 10 tokens = milk.

2. Recognise all coins.

Medium ability:

1. Cost of shop items are rounded, e.g. £1, £2.

2. Introduce place value.

High ability:

1. Cost of shop items include decimals, e.g. £1.34, £2.79.

2. Use of multiplication, e.g. one raisin = 5p therefore seven raisins = 7 x 5p = 35p.

3. Shopping list calculated mentally.

4. Weighing scales can be introduced.

Tips

1. A designated area can be set up as the shop so that the children can view all items for sale during the week. This will help focus their behaviour.

2. Do not include just one of a certain item, e.g. a board game, as this will cause frustration for the children. So, if you have 12 children in the class ensure there are 12 of everything.

3. Clear out your attic! You'll be surprised by the items you'll find which will be ideal for your shop.

4. Ask what items the children would like in their shop.

Top Shop Shopping Lists

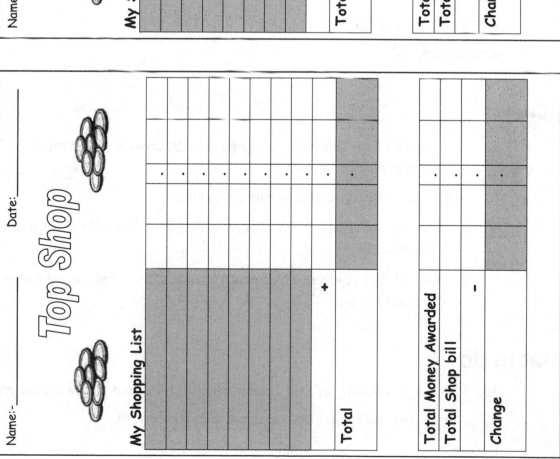

Name:- _____ Date: _____

Top Shop

My Shopping List

				·					
Total								+	

Total Money Awarded			·	
Total Shop bill			·	−
Change			·	

Name:- _____ Date: _____

Top Shop

My Shopping List

				·					
Total								+	

Total Money Awarded			·	
Total Shop bill			·	−
Change			·	

Copyright © Nicola S. Morgan 2009

Star Tokens

Star Tokens are another alternative for token rewards to help keep the children focused and interested. These are suitable for classes of all sizes and levels of behaviour. According to the class behaviour and size, the tokens are used just for a day (moderate to severe behaviour) or for a week (mild behaviour).

Aim

Help maintain and improve focus and behaviour in lessons.

Suitable for

Suitable for classes of all sizes and levels of behaviour.

What you need

- Photocopy and laminate a bundle of Star Tokens.
- Main reward.

Rules

1. Reward with Star Tokens for every positive behaviour you witness, however incidental it may be, reward it!

2. If the child displays inappropriate behaviour:

   - They do not receive a Star Token at that time, but reward for future good behaviour.

   - If the child has not received enough tokens, they will forego the end of day main reward.

What to do

1. Photocopy a bundle of Star Tokens which can be used to reward the children.

2. Decide how many Star Tokens equal the main reward.

3. Reward good behaviour with Star Tokens:

   - When you collect the children from the playground inform them of the end of day main reward and if they walk correctly to class and sit down quietly they will be given, e.g. three Star Tokens.

   - At the beginning of each lesson inform the children how many Star Tokens they will be awarded for completing each task.

   - Before the children leave the classroom for playtime inform the children that walking quietly, lining up correctly and good behaviour will be rewarded with Star Tokens.

4. Inform the children that they need to collect x Star Tokens to be rewarded the main reward.

Tips

1. Using the blank Star Tokens template let the children design their own Star Tokens.

Sample Star Tokens

Photocopy on coloured paper or allow the children to colour in and then laminate.

Marble Mania

Marble Mania is another effective way to keep children on task. This reward scheme is very popular with classes of all sizes and levels of behaviour. It is also an ideal way to keep a child focused during one-to-one sessions. Marbles can be replaced with other items such as counters or small plastic toys in order to help maintain children's interest.

Aim

Help maintain and improve focus and behaviour in lessons.

Suitable for

Small groups of children can have a jar each. Large groups of children can have a jar per table.

What you need

- Correct number of jars, which are numbered.
- Marbles.
- Correct number of larger containers.
- Marble Mania Chart.
- Main reward.

Rules

1. Reward with marbles for every positive behaviour you witness, however incidental it may be, reward it!

2. If the child displays inappropriate behaviour:

   - They do not receive any more marbles.

   - If they have not received enough marbles, they are excluded from the end of day, week and month prize.

What to do

1. Explain to the children that throughout the day they will be awarded marbles for good behaviour. This token reward process helps focus the children.

    *   At the end of the day whoever has over x amount of marbles wins the main reward, e.g. extra play.

    *   At the end of the day the table/child's marbles are placed into a larger container and the total is recorded on the Marble Mania Chart. At the end of the week whoever has over x amount of marbles wins a prize, e.g. a tea party.

2. Reward good behaviour with a marble:

    *   When you collect the children from the playground inform them of the prize (at the end of the day, week or month) and if they walk correctly to class and sit down quietly they will be given, e.g. two marbles.

    *   At the beginning of each lesson inform the children how many marbles they will be awarded for completing each task.

    *   Before the children leave the classroom for playtime inform the children that walking quietly, lining up correctly and other good behaviour will be rewarded with marbles.

Tips

1. Use different-coloured/sizes of marbles for different points, e.g. a red marble equals two points.

2. Write down different prizes and place them in envelopes labelled A, B and C. The child/table with the most marbles chooses an envelope and everyone who achieved over x marbles is rewarded that prize.

3. Record the child/table's total marbles per day on a chart which can be displayed in the classroom. This will help motivate and sustain the children's attention.

Marble Mania Tally Sheet

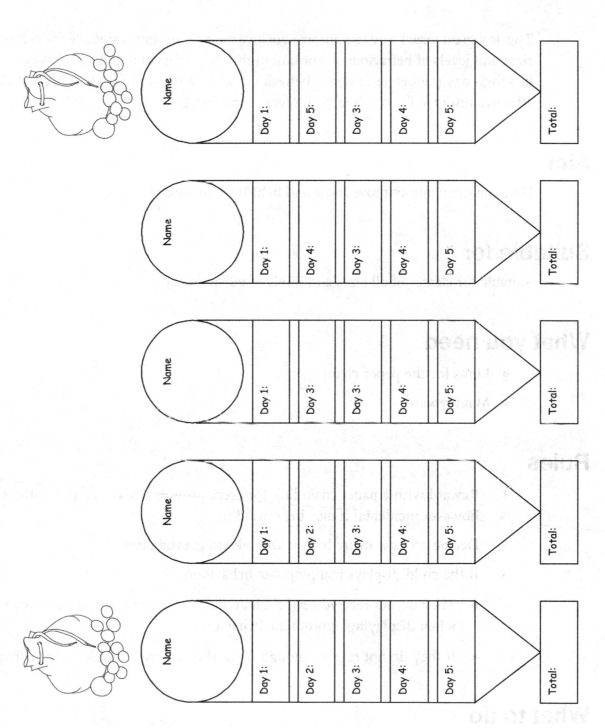

Name

| Day 1: | Day 5: | Day 3: | Day 4: | Day 5: | Total: |

Name

| Day 1: | Day 4: | Day 3: | Day 4: | Day 5: | Total: |

Name

| Day 1: | Day 3: | Day 3: | Day 4: | Day 5: | Total: |

Name

| Day 1: | Day 2: | Day 3: | Day 4: | Day 5: | Total: |

Name

| Day 1: | Day 2: | Day 3: | Day 4: | Day 5: | Total: |

Paper Chain Race

This is a great visual way to reinforce positive behaviours and is suitable for classes of all sizes and levels of behaviour. According to the class behaviour and size this can be used just for a day (moderate to severe behaviour) or for a week (mild behaviour). This is an effective resource for children with severe behaviours.

Aim

Help maintain and improve focus and behaviour in lessons.

Suitable for

Suitable for classes of all sizes and levels of behaviour.

What you need

- Links for the paper chain.
- Main reward.

Rules

1. Reward with a paper chain link for every positive behaviour you witness; however incidental it may be, reward it!

2. Decide on how many links it will take to get the prize.

3. If the child displays inappropriate behaviour:

   - They do not receive a paper chain link at that time, but reward again when displaying appropriate behaviour.

   - If they do not receive enough links, they are excluded from the prize.

What to do

1. Cut up a bundle of paper chain links which can be used to reward the children.

2. For a small group pair up the children and for a large group put the children in teams then give each team a colour, e.g. Team A = red. Place a link of each coloured paper chain high on the wall in the classroom. Each team collects as many paper chain links as they can, attaches them to the appropriate coloured link on the wall until the winner is the team which attaches the last link which touches the floor.

3. Reward good behaviour with a paper chain link:

    *   When you collect the children from the playground inform them of the prize at the end of the day and if they walk correctly to class and sit down quietly they will be given, e.g. two paper chain links.

    *   At the beginning of each lesson inform the children how many paper chain links they will be awarded for completing each task.

    *   Before the children leave the classroom for playtime inform the children that walking quietly, lining up correctly and good behaviour will be rewarded with paper chain links.

4. To avoid disruption at the end of every lesson the children, in turn, attach their links to the paper chain (the teacher may need to assist).

5. Inform the children that the more paper chain links they are rewarded the greater the chance they have to win.

Tips

1. Children can estimate the number of paper chain links it will take to reach the other side of the room and this can be discussed at the end of the competition.

2. Use scrap paper to create the chains.

3. Always give the rest of the class a small prize to reward them for their efforts.

Paper Tokens

These are another alternative for token rewards to help keep the children focused and interested. The children can create their own design on the tokens. This is suitable for classes of all sizes and levels of behaviour. According to the class behaviour and size the tokens are used just for a day (moderate to severe behaviour) or for a week (mild behaviour).

Token	Token
Token	Token
Token	Token
Token	Token

Circle Time

Circle time is a group activity designed to develop children's self-esteem and self-confidence. It provides opportunities for children to learn skills needed for effective communication and managing conflict and anger. Circle Time is not about reprimand, correction or coercion but about listening, understanding and development.

Aims

- Develop children's self-esteem and self-confidence.
- Promote and reinforce positive behaviour both inside and outside the classroom.
- Create a respectful and caring class and school atmosphere.

Suitable for

Large and small groups of children.

What you need

Enough space for all children to form a complete circle.

Rules

For children:

1. Respect all contributions made.
2. Hands up if a child wants to speak.
3. Take it in turns to speak, listen to others and do not interrupt.
4. A child can "pass" on anything they do not want to talk about.

For teacher:

1. Do not start Circle Time unless the children know how to sit, listen and contribute sensibly.
2. Start the session in a calm and relaxed way.

3.   Join in the session as a facilitator.

4.   If the chosen child is talking do not interrupt them.

5.   Respect, accept and value all contributions.

6.   Do not discuss subjects which may be sensitive or upsetting to certain children. Inform parents of the topics of Circle Time to ensure the child's well-being.

7.   End the session if the above rules for the children are continually broken. At an appropriate time the class must then discuss what they can do to ensure this doesn't happen again.

What to do

1.   Sit the children in a complete circle so that they can all see each other. The class teacher also sits within the circle and acts as a facilitator.

2.   An object can be used to pass around the circle and when a child is holding it they are allowed to speak, or instead of using an object the child's name can be called.

3.   Use token rewards to reinforce desirable behaviours during Circle Time:

   • If the children find it difficult to listen when another child is talking reward them with, for example, plastic money when they listen.

   • If a child puts their hand up and asks a question.

   • If a child sits without fidgeting.

   • If positive comments are made by a child.

4.   Subjects discussed in Circle Time must help the children explore their feelings, emotions and relationships. If negative comments occur, direct the class into positive solutions or outcomes. Use Circle Time to explore key issues that need to be addressed, for example inappropriate behaviour in the playground.

5.   Ideas to begin Circle Time:

   • Play a guessing game to help bring the group together.

   • Discuss:

      ◦ Your best day or worst day.

      ◦ Likes and dislikes.

      ◦ Goals and achievements.

    ◦   Wishes and dreams.

    ◦   What they would like to change about their behaviour.

- Show and Tell. Encourage the children to bring into school for Circle Time something which they find interesting to Show and Tell the class about.

6. Conclude Circle Time by reading a short story, poem, listening to a piece of music – anything to make sure that the children understand that the activity has come to an end.

Tips

1. If a child talks out of turn it is often because they are afraid they will not be given the opportunity to speak, therefore ensure adequate opportunities are given for everyone to speak.

2. In the early stages it is more effective to have mini circle times after every break-time to help reinforce good behaviours and discuss solutions to inappropriate behaviours.

3. For effective results operate Circle Time at the same time every week.

Stickers

Children respond well to stickers and they are a quick and easy reward to deliver to reinforce positive behaviours. Stickers are suitable for classes of all sizes and levels of behaviour.

Aim

Help maintain and improve focus and behaviour in lessons.

Suitable for

Suitable for classes of all sizes and levels of behaviour.

What you need

- Variety of different stickers.
- Marble Mania Chart.
- Main reward.

Rules

1. Reward with stickers for every positive behaviour you witness; however incidental it may be, reward it!

2. If the child displays inappropriate behaviour:

   - They do not receive a sticker at that time, but reward for future good behaviour.

   - If the child has not received enough stickers, they forego the end of day main reward.

What to do

1. Explain to the children that throughout the day they will be awarded stickers for good behaviour. This token reward process helps focus the children.

Create a system for using different types of stickers to represent different levels of achievement so that children know what they are aiming for.

- Throughout the day children will be rewarded with different stickers for good behaviour.

- At the end of the day whoever has x amount of stickers receives the main reward (decide how many stickers equal the main reward).

2. Reward good behaviour with a sticker:

- When you collect the children from the playground inform them of the main reward and if they walk correctly to class and sit down quietly they will be given a sticker.

- At the beginning of each lesson inform the children how many stickers they will be awarded for completing each task.

- Before the children leave the classroom for playtime inform the children that walking quietly, lining up correctly and good behaviour will be rewarded with stickers.

Tips

1. Provide each child with a sticker book so that they can keep a record of their stickers.

2. Record the child/table's total stickers per day on a chart which can be displayed in the classroom. This will help motivate and sustain the children's focus.

Free Time

The Free Time reward is suitable for classes of all sizes and levels of behaviour. This is a great reward to give to a child, for example when they have completed a piece of work. It keeps them focused and on task knowing that they can have time to choose their own activity. For small groups free time can be used as a main reward at the end of the day for all children to choose an activity.

Aim

To maintain the children's behaviour and help focus them on tasks set throughout the day.

Suitable for

Suitable for classes of all sizes and levels of behaviour.

What you need

- Board games, puzzles.
- Art and craft materials.
- Computer games.
- Quiet reading area.

Rules

1. Give the children token rewards throughout the day. When they have received *x* amount of token rewards (decide on the amount each day) they are rewarded with Free Time which can last between five and 15 minutes depending on the children.

2. If the child displays inappropriate behaviour:

   - They do not receive a token reward at that time, but reward for future good behaviour.

   - If they haven't received enough token rewards, they forego the Free Time.

3. When the child has Free Time they must choose one activity. Inform the children that if they choose an activity then change their mind they forfeit their Free Time. This eliminates fussing and disagreements.

What to do

1. Explain to the children that throughout the day they will be awarded token rewards for good behaviour.

   - When a child has received x amount of token rewards they are rewarded with Free Time, they are provided with a few options, e.g. play a board game.

2. Create designated Free Time stations around the classroom so that when children are in Free Time they do not distract the children who are still working.

3. Explain each Free Time activity to the children, e.g. if they choose to make a model car go through the construction process with them or provide them with simple step by step pictorial instructions.

4. Inform the children how many children per area, e.g. only two children on the computer.

Tips

1. Make each Free Time station interesting.

2. Choose activities which the children enjoy, e.g. a Top Trump card area.

3. Change the Free Time activities every week.

4. For children who find it difficult to stay on task, the Free Time Reward works well. For these children instead of them collecting 10 token rewards for 10 minutes of Free Time allow them to collect five token rewards for five minutes of Free Time.

Extra Play

Extra Play is suitable for classes of all sizes and levels of behaviour. For large classes it can be used, for example, if all children have completed a set task. Here, the teacher takes them out to play 5–10 minutes before or after playtime. For small classes, e.g. ten children, Extra Play can be used as an end of day main reward.

Aim

To maintain the children's behaviour and help focus them on tasks set throughout the day.

Suitable for

Suitable for classes of all sizes and levels of behaviour.

What you need

- Sport equipment, e.g. football, tennis racquets.
- Arts and crafts, e.g. sketch pads.
- Small cones.
- Whistle.

Rules

1. If the child displays inappropriate behaviour:

    - They do not receive a token reward at that time, but reward future good behaviour.

    - If they have not received enough token rewards, they forego Extra Play.

2. If a child displays inappropriate behaviour during Extra Play they are removed from the playground and do not receive the treat when they return to the class.

What to do

1. Reward the children with token rewards throughout the day. When they have received x amount of token rewards (decide on the number to achieve each day) they are rewarded with Extra Play which can take place at the end of the playtime in the afternoon.

2. Create designated Extra Play stations around the playground so that the children have their own space to enjoy their activity.

3. Inform them how many per area/activity.

4. To ensure all children return to class in a sensible fashion have a small treat ready for them, e.g. milk and squash.

Tips

1. Make each Extra Play station interesting.

2. Choose activities which the children enjoy.

3. Change the Extra Play activities every week.

4. If the children choose to play a team game, e.g. football, the teacher must become the referee and inform the children of the rules when playing. If these types of activities are not monitored they can sometimes lead to displays of inappropriate behaviours.

Breakfast Club

Suitable for small classes, e.g. ten children, and all levels of behaviour. Breakfast Club is especially helpful for those children who come to school on an empty stomach. Providing a simple breakfast helps to maintain the right behaviour and create a positive mood.

Aims

- Help maintain and improve focus and behaviour in lessons.
- Improve attendance and time-keeping.
- Impact on mental performance.
- Develop a positive, happy mood.

Suitable for

Suitable for small classes, e.g. ten children and all levels of behaviour.

What you need

Healthy breakfast. Check children's dietary requirements and allergies.

Rules

1. The child forfeits eating breakfast with their friends if they displayed inappropriate behaviour before breakfast club begins, e.g. walked into school displaying inappropriate behaviour. The inappropriately-behaved child should take a Time Out before receiving breakfast.

What to do

1. Set up the breakfast club every morning and encourage the children to help.
2. Vary the type of food and drink available for each breakfast.
3. When the children are eating their breakfast encourage discussions, e.g. "What did you do on the weekend?"
4. This time can also be used for registration and Special Day, see p.70.

Tips

1. Breakfast Club can be available every day, twice a week, etc.

2. Breakfast Club can take place in the dinner hall, classroom, staff room, etc.

References

Canfield, J. (1982) 'The Limitless Power of Your Mind.' in B. Deporter and M. Hernacki (eds) (1992) *Quantum Learning*. New York, NY: Dell Publishing Company.

Skinner, B.F. (1974) *About Behaviorism*. New York, NY: Alfred A Knopf.

Smiles, S. (2002) *Self-Help*. New York, NY: Oxford Paperbacks.

Smith, P. (1993) *Professional Assault Response Training* (2000) (Revised) San Clemente, CA: Professsional Growth Facilitators.

Witte, E.H. & Davis, J.H. (1996) *Understanding Group Behaviour: Small Group Processes and Interpersonal Relations, Vol 2*. Mahwah, NJ: Lawrence Eribaum Associates.

Index